The Value of
Recreational Sports
in Higher Education

Library of Congress Cataloging-in-Publication Data

The value of recreational sports in higher education : impact on student
enrollment, success, and buying power / National Intramural-Recreational
Sports Association.
    p. cm.
Includes bibliographical references.
  ISBN 0-7360-5503-7 (softcover)
  1. College sports—Economic aspects—United States. 2. College
students—United States—Attitudes. 3. Recreational surveys—United
States. 4. Educational surveys—United States. I. National
Intramural-Recreational Sports Association (U.S.)
  GV350.V35 2004
  796.04'3'0973—dc22   2003024568

ISBN: 0-7360-5503-7

Communications Specialist Editor: Sarah Jane Hubert
Graphic Designer: Cory Granholm
Cover Designer: Andrea Souflee
Printer: Versa Press

Printed in the United States of America   10 9 8 7 6 5 4 3 2 1

Human Kinetics
Web site: www.HumanKinetics.com

United States: Human Kinetics
P.O. Box 5076
Champaign, IL 61825-5076
800-747-4457
e-mail: humank@hkusa.com

Canada: Human Kinetics
475 Devonshire Road Unit 100
Windsor, ON N8Y 2L5
800-465-7301 (in Canada only)
e-mail: orders@hkcanada.com

Europe: Human Kinetics
107 Bradford Road
Stanningley
Leeds LS28 6AT, United Kingdom
+44 (0) 113 255 5665
e-mail: hk@hkeurope.com

Australia: Human Kinetics
57A Price Avenue
Lower Mitcham, South Australia 5062
08 8277 1555
e-mail: liaw@hkaustralia.com

New Zealand: Human Kinetics
Division of Sports Distributors NZ Ltd.
P.O. Box 300 226 Albany
North Shore City
Auckland
0064 9 448 1207
e-mail: blairc@hknewz.com

The Value of Recreational Sports in Higher Education

Contents

Foreword

As the National Intramural-Recreational Sports Association (NIRSA) continues to emphasize the importance of campus recreation for students to college and university administrators, the Association has taken that commitment one step farther. NIRSA and its publishing partner, Human Kinetics, have collaborated to print this book, *The Value of Recreational Sports in Higher Education.* It combines the first, second, and third sections of the 2002 Kerr & Downs Research Report (K-D) commissioned by the NIRSA Board of Directors. The first section of the research report appeared in the 2003 Spring Issue of the *Recreational Sports Journal.*

It confirms what NIRSA members have always known: that participation in recreational sports programs and activities is a key determinant of college satisfaction, success, recruitment, and retention. While these students are concerned about the same academic standards and quality of education as other students, they are more likely to succeed at college and be more satisfied with the experience. The report cites that the top benefits of recreational sports programs include: improves emotional well-being, reduces stress, and improves happiness. Recreational sports programs build self-confidence and character, promote diversity, teach team building, and improve leadership skills.

The second section of the K-D report deals with the results of an expenditure survey, and the third section goes into the specific statistics of the actual buying power of recreational sports participants. This information will be invaluable to purveyors of recreational sports equipment and services who present at trade shows.

Architectural and planning firms that plan and bid on indoor/outdoor recreational facilities will want to see the list of those surveyed schools that plan to build new facilities or renovate older ones listed in the Appendix Section.

This book will be of interest not only to recreational sports professionals and students who serve within higher education, but also to other industry-related associations and other college/university campus departments such as: Admissions, Campus Activities, Planning, Capital Fund-Raising, Resident Halls, Student Unions, and Student Governing Associations.

As a textbook for college/university courses in Recreation and Leisure Studies, Recreational Management, Sports Management, and Sports Marketing academic departments, it will reveal not only the many facets associated with this industry, but its future trends as well.

Kent J. Blumental, PhD
NIRSA Executive Director
November, 2003

NIRSA - The National Intramural-Recreational Sports Association

The National Intramural-Recreational Sports Association has a rich history, and established itself as the pioneer of organized recreation, primarily for colleges and universities. Founded in 1950 at Dillard University in New Orleans by 22 African-American men and women intramural directors from 11 Historically Black Colleges, NIRSA began as the National Intramural Association (NIA). Dr. William Wasson, who convened the initial meeting, served as NIA's first president, and is revered as NIRSA's founder.

Today, NIRSA is a nonprofit membership organization serving a network of more than 4,000 highly trained professional, student, and associate members in the recreational sports field throughout the United States, Canada, and other countries. It is the leading organization in many areas: training and professional development, intramural sports, sport clubs, recreation facilities, fitness programming, outdoor recreation, wellness programs, informal recreation, and aquatic programs. Of NIRSA's 740 institutional members, 94 percent are from college and university recreational sports programs. NIRSA's member institutions represent nearly seven million college students, of whom an estimated five and a half million participate in recreational sports, fitness and wellness programs. More than 1.1 million intramural contests are scheduled annually, and more than two million individuals participate in collegiate sport clubs each year—four student athletes for every one varsity athlete.

NIRSA's Mission Statement

The mission of the National Intramural-Recreational Sports Association is to provide for the education and development of professional and student members and to foster quality recreational programs, facilities, and services for diverse populations. NIRSA demonstrates its commitment to excellence by utilizing resources that promote ethical and healthy lifestyle choices.

NIRSA National Center, 4185 SW Research Way, Corvallis, Oregon 97330-1067
Telephone: (541) 766-8211, Fax: (541) 766-8284, Website: www.nirsa.org

Section I

The Value of Recreational Sports on College Campuses

Introduction

Purpose

Kerr & Downs Research* conducted this research study for the National Intramural-Recreational Sports Association (NIRSA). The purpose of this study was three-fold:

1. To examine the value and contribution of recreational sports to participants' lives
2. To determine the economic impact of NIRSA member colleges and universities
3. To document the buying power of participants of recreational sports

Because a significant percentage of NIRSA's member organizations are colleges and universities, this study focused on participants of recreational sports on college and university campuses. While faculty and individuals who are not students utilize campus recreational sports facilities, this study focuses on students. Participants of college recreational sports programs and activities include the following:

- Organized recreational teams and league sports participants
- Fitness class participants
- Workout center/recreation center programs
- Exercise enthusiasts
- Organized sports clubs
- Aquatic enthusiasts
- Outdoor recreation enthusiasts
- Other participants in recreational sports and fitness programs, services and facilities

---

*Project Director: Phillip E. Downs, Ph.D., 2992 Habersham Drive, Tallahassee, FL 32309, (850) 906-3111, www.kerr-downs.com

Value and Contribution

This study focuses on the value of recreational sports to college students by focusing on self-report measures such as:

1. The relative importance of recreational sports participation as a determinant of college satisfaction and success vis-à-vis other determinants
2. The extent to which students identified recreational sports facilities and programs as a priority for receiving college resources and funding
3. Happiness with college experiences and life
4. Perceived benefits of participation in recreational sports programs and activities
5. The relationship between recreational sports participation and positive behaviors (e.g., hours devoted to community service) and negative behaviors (e.g., smoking cigarettes)
6. Academic measures such as grade point average and academic hours taken

Contributors to the Study

While Kerr & Downs Research accepts responsibility for limitations of the study related to methodology and implementation, many individuals made significant contributions to this research effort. NIRSA members Sid Gonsoulin, director of Recreational Sports at the University of Southern Mississippi, John Meyer, associate director of Recreational Sports at the University of Colorado, and Aaron Hill, marketing director for NIRSA, worked extensively with Kerr & Downs Research throughout the study. Without their direction and hands-on efforts, the study would not have been completed.

We also wish to thank the 2000-2001 year NIRSA board of directors that were in office during the planning and implementation of most of this research effort:

- Patti Bostic, President
- Bill Sells, Past President
- Brian Carswell, President-Elect
- Patricia R. Besner, Past Presidents' Representative
- Warren Isenhour, National Student Representative
- Kent Blumenthal, Executive Director
- Jeffrey S. Kearney, Region I Vice President
- Sid Gonsoulin, Region II Vice President
- Jan Wells, Region III Vice President
- Warren Simpson, Region IV Vice President
- Ron Seibring, Region V Vice President
- Kathleen Hatch, Region VI Vice President

Sincere appreciation is also extended to a Senior Advisory Group. These individuals contributed their expertise toward sample composition and questionnaire issues:

- Judith Bryant
- Jesse Clements
- Mary Daniels
- Michael Deluca
- William Ehling
- Mark Fletcher
- Janet Gong
- William Healey
- Thomas Kirch
- Gerald Maas
- John Meyer
- Eric Nickel
- James Turman
- Jeffrey Vessely

A special thank you is due to the campus recreation directors at the sixteen colleges involved in the study. These individuals facilitated data collection, and thus made the study possible:

- Ned Britt
- Bill Canning
- Scott Campbell
- Tony Clements
- Rob Frye
- Kathleen Hatch
- Greg Jordan
- Jan Maguire
- Judy Muencho
- Maureen McGonagle
- Norm Parsons
- Butch Sutton
- Pamela Su
- Art Tuveson
- Tina Villard
- Pam Wetherbee-Metcalf

Research Method

For pragmatic reasons, a cross-sectional research design was selected for this study. The goal was to collect self-report data on the value of recreational sports to participants and the buying power of participants from a representative sample of students at NIRSA member colleges.

To operationalize this goal, elements of cluster and systematic random sampling techniques were utilized. The concept of cluster sampling was first applied by selecting sixteen colleges based on the following criteria: student enrollment, geographic location, public vs. private, urban setting vs. rural setting, and four-year vs. two-year institution. The objective was to select sixteen colleges that collectively would enable exposure to a representative sample of college students. A pragmatic criterion of college selection was the ability to obtain approval from recreational sports departments and college officials within a limited time frame for conducting interviews with students on campus.

Based on these criteria, the following colleges were selected and graciously agreed to participate:

- Bridgewater State College
- Colorado State University
- DePaul University
- Florida International University
- Loyola College (Baltimore)
- Oakland University
- Regis College
- Rice University
- San Jacinto College
- Sonoma State University
- Towson University
- University of Illinois
- University of Miami
- University of Michigan
- University of Rhode Island
- Washington State University

To ensure that representative samples of students were selected at each college, the goal was to designate six to ten points on each campus that would give interviewers exposure to a representative mix of students on that campus. Because of weather, college-imposed constraints and operational difficulties, the actual number of data collection locations on campuses ranged from three to ten.

Interviewers were stationed at selected points on campuses and instructed to systematically select students as they passed. There were three or four interviewers on each campus. Interviewers often collected data at several points on campus throughout the interviewing period that normally lasted six to eight hours.

A total of 2,673 interviews were completed across the sixteen campuses during February, 2002. The sampling error given a 95 percent confidence level was ±1.9 percent.

Research designed to examine the value of recreational sports to participants and the buying power of participants can employ a longitudinal or cross-sectional methodology. The former was not utilized because of time constraints. Methodology that measures value and buying power for an ongoing process such as recreational sports at one point in time provides information for a given point in time and relies on self-reported data.

Executive Summary

The National Intramural-Recreational Sports Association (NIRSA) study on the impact of participation in recreational sports programs and activities on college* campuses discovered several key relationships between participation and college and personal success factors. This study represents the most comprehensive attempt to investigate the impact of participation in recreational sports programs and activities on college satisfaction and performance. More than 2,600 students from sixteen (16) colleges participated in this study making it the largest, representative group of college students from multiple colleges ever studied with respect to the value of participation in recreational sports.

Other researchers have studied the value of recreational sports on college campuses. Most of these studies have focused on one specific college. Findings of these studies are summarized in the next section of this report.

College Satisfaction and Success

The NIRSA study found that participation in recreational sports programs and activities is correlated with overall college satisfaction and success. Participation in recreational sports is an important determinant of overall college satisfaction and success. While some determinants of satisfaction and success in college were more critical than recreational sports (such as academic courses, professors, job/graduate school prospects, housing and transportation), this study, nonetheless, reinforced what other limited research on this issue has found: namely that participation in recreational sports is a key determinant of satisfaction and success in college.

The NIRSA study showed convincingly that heavy users** of campus recreational sports programs and activities were happier than light users** and nonusers**. Further, the study showed that students who participated in recreational

---

* The term "college" will be used throughout to refer to colleges and universities. ** For analysis purposes, students were grouped into three groups: (1) heavy users of recreational sports programs and activities – students who participated at least 25 times a month, (2) light users – students who participated up to 25 times per month, and (3) nonusers. Heavy users comprised 21% of the students, light users comprised 54% of the students and nonusersrepresented 25% of students.

sports programs and activities identified recreational sports as one of the key determinants of college satisfaction and success. For example, recreational sports programs and activities was the fifth (out of 21 factors) most significant determinant of college satisfaction and success for heavy users. Among all students, recreational sports programs and activities ranked higher than internships, cultural activities, part-time or full-time work, student clubs and organizations, shopping, entertainment, restaurant options in the community, chance to study abroad, community service opportunities, watching varsity sports, participating in varsity sports, and sororities/fraternities as determinants of college satisfaction and success.

The importance of participation in recreational sports programs and activities was rather consistent across students' undergraduate experiences, yet it was slightly more important to freshmen and male students. There was not an appreciable drop in the importance of participation in recreational sports as a determinant of college satisfaction and success even among graduate students. The value of participation in recreational sports held for students at public and private colleges and for students at small and large colleges although the value at small colleges was slightly less.

Heavy users of recreational sports programs and activities were similar to other students in the importance they placed in quality and range of courses, quality of professors, and graduate school/job prospects as determinants of college satisfaction and success. In other words, heavy participants in recreational sports were serious students concerned about the same academic standards and quality of education as other students. Heavy users simply were happier than other students and found recreational sports programs and activities to be more important in determining the overall value of their college experiences.

Students who participated heavily in college recreational sports programs and activities were more socially oriented than other students. For example, they placed more importance on sororities/fraternities, student clubs and organizations, meeting new and different people, and social activities. They were also more interested in watching or participating in varsity sports compared to other students. Finally, heavy users of recreational sports programs and activities rated diversity of the student population as a more important determinant of their college satisfaction and success than did other students.

Allocating College Resources

Students preferred that more college money be spent on professors, technology, libraries, housing and classrooms. Recreational sports programs and activities ranked below these aforementioned priorities, yet above campus organizations and clubs, campus landscaping and beautification, recruiting students, and varsity athletic programs. Among heavy users of recreational sports programs and activities (21% of the students) recreational sports programs and activities ranked third as a target for more funding. Only technology and professors were more critical targets for additional funding.

Identifying recreational sports programs and activities as a priority for funding did not vary considerably across class level, gender or race/ethnicity. Students at public and private colleges did not vary in their feelings about the priority of recreational sports as a target for more funding. Students at medium-sized colleges were more likely to identify recreational sports programs and activities as a priority for more funding.

Benefits of Participation

Students agreed that participating in recreational sports resulted in the following wide range of benefits (in priority order):

1. Improves emotional well-being
2. Reduces stress
3. Improves happiness
4. Improves self-confidence
5. Builds character
6. Makes students feel like part of the college community
7. Improves interaction with diverse sets of people
8. Is an important part of college social life
9. Teaches team-building skills
10. Is an important part of the learning experience
11. Aids in time management
12. Improves leadership skills

There was a direct correlation between the level of participation and the degree to which students received the benefits listed above. For example, heavy users of recreational sports were more likely to agree that participation improved their overall emotional well-being. This relationship was true for participation and all benefits. Benefits of participation in recreational sports were greater to students during their first three years in college and dropped slightly during their senior year and graduate school. Benefits of recreational sports were equally strong for males and females and stronger for African Americans, Hispanics and whites, and somewhat lower among Asian students.

In general, students at public and private colleges had similar perceptions of the benefits of recreational sports. Students at public colleges were more likely to agree that participation increased their self-confidence, while students at private colleges were more likely to agree that participation helped them feel that they were part of the college community. Students at medium- sized colleges were more likely than students at small or large colleges to perceive the value of participation in recreational sports.

Positive and Negative Behaviors

Participation in recreational sports programs and activities was directly correlated with positive behaviors such as community service, not smoking, attending religious services and heavier course loads (number of hours taken per term). However, participation in recreational sports programs and activities was also directly correlated to negative behaviors such as alcohol and illegal drug consumption, missing school or work and cheating in college. Other studies have shown that participants are more likely to be risk takers and are more socially oriented (also supported by NIRSA's study), and these characteristics are correlated with behaviors such as alcohol and illegal drug consumption.

There was no relationship between percentage of college expenses paid and participation in recreational sports programs and activities. SAT scores of participants were slightly higher than those of nonparticipants, yet there was no relationship between ACT scores and participation in recreational sports. Differences in grade point averages (GPAs) across heavy, light and nonuser groups were virtually nonexistent. Other studies have shown a positive correlation between participation and grades.

Previous Research on the Value of Recreational Sports on College Campuses

The majority of the literature on intramural and recreational sports participation has focused on participants' personality characteristics, college satisfaction, scholastic achievement, attrition rates and recruitment. Although recreational sports research is in an infantile stage, with few formal studies, the research to date* points to many positive correlations about the qualities of participants and benefits of participation.

College Satisfaction

One of the most consistent findings in recreational research is that student satisfaction is highly correlated with extracurricular involvement, specifically in intramural and recreational sports. In a four-year follow-up study of intercollegiate athletes, intramural athletes and nonathletes, Ryan found that "Participation in intramural sports appears to have a positive effect on student retention, degree aspirations and satisfaction with the college experience" (Ryan, 1990, page 100). In fact, intramural sports participation was found to be one of the strongest in-college activity predictors of overall college satisfaction, along with election to student office, getting good grades, and holding a part-time job on campus. The study also showed that intramural and recreational sports participants were among the two student groups less likely to feel overwhelmed (along with those with higher GPAs) (page 47).

Consistent with Ryan's findings, research from Harvard University concluded the following:

> Substantial commitment to one or two activities other than course work - for as much as 20 to 30 hours per week - has little or no relationship to grades. Such commitments do have a strong relationship to overall satisfaction with college life. More involvement is strongly correlated with higher satisfaction. (Light, 1990, page 41).

---

* See bibliography section at the end of this publication for resources cited.

In Smith and Thomas' study of recent alumni of the University of Tennessee, participation in intramurals was correlated to several other factors. Smith and Thomas found:

> Two variables — relationships with faculty and participation in intramurals — had the most positive correlations… Engaging in intramurals could predict salary, feeling positively about pay in your job, satisfaction with educational experiences then and now, and satisfaction with your present social and cultural experiences. (Smith and Thomas, 1989, page 12).

Astin (1984), Ryan (1990) and Varca, Shaffer and Sanders (1984) have all concluded that participation in athletic pursuits is related to student satisfaction (Astin, 1984). Bucholz' 1993 study of graduate and undergraduate students at Arizona State University showed that freshmen Sport Recreation Center users scored higher on perceived benefit in personal development than nonusers. Also in 1993, Ragheb, and McKinney supported their hypothesis that "the more students participate in recreation activities, the less they perceive stress." (page 5).

Recruitment and Retention

Another benefit of college involvement and thus satisfaction is retention. Many studies have shown that what happens when one enters and becomes a part of a college environment is more indicative of their persistence at college than pre-entry occurrences (Pascarella & Terenzini, 1977, Terenzini & Pascarella, 1977). Participation in collegiate sports and utilization of recreational facilities have repeatedly been found as two of the biggest factors in college persistence (Maas, 1999; Ryan, 1990). According to Wade, "establishing membership and a sense of belonging in a community is a critical component of retention" (Wade, 1991 page 7).

In a study at Arizona State University, Maas studied persistence rates of college freshmen who were users and nonusers of the university's Student Recreation Complex (SRC). The major finding was that persistence rates for SRC users "clearly outpaced that of their nonuser counterparts" (Belch, Gebel & Maas, page 261). Using different scales such as ACT scores, SAT scores, college GPA and high school GPA, Maas also compared students' academic credentials. "It appears that SRC users are, as a group, less academically qualified than nonusers, but are retained in higher numbers." (Maas, page 14).

Astin's research concurred that involvement in cocurricular activities significantly contributes to persistence (Astin 1975, 1977, 1993).

Intramural and recreational sports also have a strong influence on student recruitment. A telephone survey of 500 prospective students was conducted and published in "Student Poll," Vol. 4, No.4 by Art and Science Group. The major findings of the poll included:

1. Intramural and recreational sports have a much greater influence on college choice than intercollegiate athletics (page 1).
2. Even among male respondents, intramural sports were a more important factor in college choice than intercollegiate sports (page 3).

Personality

The range of personality characteristics that have been consistently found in intramural participants as opposed to nonparticipants is wide. In a 1942 study, Sperling compared varsity athletes, intramural athletes and nonathletes at a New York City college, finding superiority in adjustment scores, emotional stability and extraversion as distinguishing characteristics of the varsity and intramural athlete groups from the nonathletes. Higher social adjustment scores among intramural and varsity athletes, as opposed to their nonathletic counterparts, have also been presented in research of Biddulph (1954) and Booth (1958). Sperling's study also found no significant difference in personality traits between the intramural and varsity athlete groups (Sperling 1942).

In 1963, Ryan conducted a six-month study of male college freshmen, dividing subjects into an experimental and control group, to determine the effects of intramural participation on an individual's personality. Although the results failed to show a statistically significant difference between the two groups, five of the six traits measured increased in favor of the participating group (page 51). These traits included: sociability, confidence, home satisfaction, analytic thinking and personal relations. Ryan suggested future studies be conducted over a longer period of time than the six-month period used in this study citing the study's length as a possible explanation for the lack of statistically significant difference in personality between the two groups.

Mendell's 1973 dissertation compares personalities of male intramural sports participants to nonparticipants (page 3). Mendell found the intramural or athletic participant to be more happy-go-lucky, venturesome, tough minded, suspicious, practical and conservative. These findings seem congruent with those of Sperling, Werner and Gottheil, Kroll and Petersen, Merriman and Ryan. Contrary to Mendell's conclusion that athletes are more "group-dependent," Astin (1968) and Werner and Gottheil (1966) found high levels of independence and self-sufficiency among athletes.

Scholastic Achievement

Hackensmith and Miller's study of intramural activity participants and nonparticipants at the University of Kentucky showed intramural participants with a higher mean intelligence sigma ranking as opposed to nonparticipants (1930). In a late 1960s study of first-year college men, Berg discovered that intramural sports participants had a significantly higher level of academic achievement than nonparticipants. He also found greater participation in intramural sports from those with higher academic ability (1970). After surveying athletic participation and scholastic achievement in his own study, Rarick hypothesized that high-quality students are highly involved in collegiate intramurals (1943).

In a 2001 report from Washington State University, data from student card operations and the institution's Data Warehouse were combined to show relationships between various elements and Student Recreation Center (SRC) use. One of the most consistent findings was the positive relationship between grade point average (GPA) and frequency of SRC use. For every semester (spring, summer and fall), both grade point averages (GPAs) and average credit hours taken were higher for students who entered the SRC at least once than for those who never entered the SRC.

Freshmen who entered the SRC more than 30 times during the spring semester had an average GPA of 2.85, followed by a 2.56 GPA for those who entered 1-10 times and a 2.47 GPA for those who never entered the SRC. Additionally, in spring and fall terms, students were divided into 10 percent intervals based on their frequency of SRC use. Frequent users of the SRC (top 10%) had higher GPAs than any other group (Washington State University).

However, other studies on intramural sports participants have either failed to show a relationship between participation and academic achievement (Mendell) or found a negative relationship between the two (Ryan, page 100).

Value of Recreational Sports on College Campuses

Determinants of College Satisfaction & Success

Students were asked to indicate how important each of 21 factors was in affecting their overall satisfaction and success in college. Each factor was evaluated on a 10-point scale where 1 indicated total lack of importance and 10 indicated very high importance. For example, if participating in recreational sports was a very important part of a student's overall satisfaction and success in college, a score of 8 or 9, or even 10 would be assigned to participation in recreational sports. Conversely, if student clubs and organizations were not an important part of a student's overall satisfaction and success in college, a score of 1, 2 or 3 would be assigned to student clubs and organizations.

The graph on page 25 summarizes the average scores (on a 10-point scale) for each of 21 factors rated by students. Course content and range of courses was the most important factor contributing to the overall satisfaction and success of college students, followed closely by quality of professors and the potential for interaction between students and professors. Prospects for jobs or graduate school were also rated highly as a contributing factor in students' overall satisfaction and success in college.

Participation in recreational sports and activities ranked 11th, exactly in the middle of the 21 factors. Recreational sports and activities barely missed being ranked seventh as six factors were bunched closely around 7.5 on the 10-point scale. Carrying the averages out to the hundredths resulted in recreational sports and activities settling in eleventh place.

There was a significant gap between the factors that were bunched in the middle (with scores of 7.3 to 7.5) and the remaining factors. Student clubs and organizations, studying abroad, participating in or watching varsity sports and sorority/fraternity/social clubs ranked considerably below recreational sports and activities as determinants of college satisfaction and success.

It is interesting to note the relative positions of recreational sports and activities and factors related to varsity sports. Participating in varsity sports ranked next to last in terms of importance in college students' overall satisfaction and

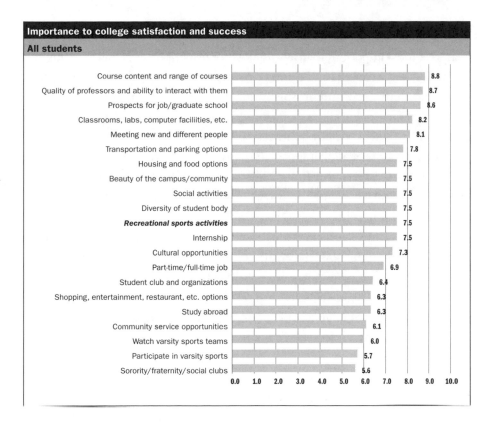

Importance to college satisfaction and success

All students

Course content and range of courses	8.8
Quality of professors and ability to interact with them	8.7
Prospects for job/graduate school	8.6
Classrooms, labs, computer facilities, etc.	8.2
Meeting new and different people	8.1
Transportation and parking options	7.8
Housing and food options	7.5
Beauty of the campus/community	7.5
Social activities	7.5
Diversity of student body	7.5
Recreational sports activities	7.5
Internship	7.5
Cultural opportunities	7.3
Part-time/full-time job	6.9
Student club and organizations	6.4
Shopping, entertainment, restaurant, etc. options	6.3
Study abroad	6.3
Community service opportunities	6.1
Watch varsity sports teams	6.0
Participate in varsity sports	5.7
Sorority/fraternity/social clubs	5.6

0.0 1.0 2.0 3.0 4.0 5.0 6.0 7.0 8.0 9.0 10.0

success. It could be argued that this low ranking is a function of the fact that most students do not participate in varsity sports. However, this argument cannot be used as successfully when considering the low ranking of watching varsity sports.

Segmentation

*Graphs on pages 30 and 31 show how heavy, light and nonusers of recreational sports and activities ranked the 21 factors. As explained in depth on page 22, heavy users (21% of students) were students who participated most frequently in recreational sports and activities; light users (54% of students) participated in recreational sports and activities, but less so than heavy users; and nonusers (25% of students) (page 23) did not participate at all in recreational sports and activities.

Heavy users ranked recreational sports and activities fifth out of the 21 factors compared to a ranking of 11th given by all students. Among heavy users, recreational sports and activities was grouped with five other factors that received average scores on the 10-point scale ranging from 8.3 to 8.7. The same factors that were most important to heavy users, were also important to all students. For example, course content and range of courses, quality of professors and ability to interact with them, and prospects for graduate school or a job were the top three rated factors for all students and for heavy users of college recreational sports and activities. Socially-related factors were comparatively more important to heavy users of recreational sports and activities. For instance, meeting new and different people ranked fourth for heavy users and fifth for all students, and social activities ranked seventh for heavy users and ninth for all students. However, sororities and fraternities ranked last for heavy users as well as for all students.

Importance of recreational sports and activities decreased as participation decreased. Light users ranked recreational sports and activities 12th, while non-users ranked recreational sports and activities 14th. It should be noted that non-users and light users, as well as heavy users had the same top three factors. That is, the importance of course content, quality faculty and prospects for jobs or graduate school did not vary based on incidence of participation in recreational sports and activities.

The table on page 31 shows how recreational sports and activities was ranked by students of varying levels of race/ethnicity, gender and level in college. Comparatively speaking, males considered recreational sports and activities to be considerably more important than females did. Recreational sports and activities was ranked sixth by males and 13th by females; yet, this result is a bit misleading. Examination of the graph on page 32 shows that males (7.5) and females (7.4) gave nearly equal averages for recreational sports and activities on a 10-point scale. Females merely gave higher scores to several other factors, which resulted in recreational sports and activities dropping to 13th.

Importance of recreational sports and activities to students' overall satisfaction and success in college did not vary much throughout college. Freshmen ranked recreational sports and activities 9th, while students at other academic levels ranked it 10th or 11th. It is interesting to note from the graph on page 32 that freshmen and sophomores gave higher ratings (7.6) to recreational sports and activities than seniors and graduate students (7.3). This result gives credence to the premise that recreational sports and activities is an important part of the bonding experience and helps younger students feel like part of the college experience.

Caucasians gave a higher ranking (9th) to recreational sports and activities compared to rankings by students of other races/ethnicities. Yet examination of the graph on page 33 shows that African Americans and Asians actually gave higher scores to recreational sports and activities than did Caucasians. Recreational sports and activities was ranked lower by these two racial/ethnic groups because they rated many other factors higher than did Caucasians.

Public vs. Private Colleges

The table on page 34 shows how students at public and private colleges ranked the 21 determinants of college satisfaction and success. Students at public colleges ranked participation in recreation eighth, while those at private colleges ranked it 12th. That is, participation in recreational sports programs and activities was relatively more critical to students' overall college satisfaction and success at public colleges.

Size of College

The table on page 29 shows the importance of the 21 factors to overall college satisfaction and success for students at small, medium and large colleges. Importance of recreational sports as a determinant of college satisfaction and success was directly correlated to size of the college. Students at large colleges ranked recreational sports seventh; students at medium sized colleges ranked it eighth; and students at small colleges ranked recreational sports 13th in terms of impacting their overall college satisfaction and success.

Graphs on pages 35 through 44 show how heavy, light and nonusers of recreational sports and activities rated all 21 determinants of college satisfaction and success. These graphs show that heavy users of campus recreational sports programs and activities are very similar to other students with certain important distinctions. Heavy users are similar to other students in the importance that the following have in determining their overall college satisfaction and success:

- Internships
- Quality of professors
- Part-time and full-time jobs during college
- Community service opportunities
- Study abroad opportunities
- Classrooms, labs, and computer facilities
- Beauty of the campus/community
- Cultural opportunities
- Course content and range of courses
- Transportation and parking options
- Shopping entertainment restaurants etc. in the community
- Diversity of the student body
- Prospects for jobs or graduate school

Yet heavy users of campus recreational sports programs and activities were different from other students in the importance that socially-oriented factors had on their overall college satisfaction and success. For example, heavy users of recreational sports programs and activities compared to other students indicated that the following were more important to their overall college satisfaction and success.

- Sororities/fraternities/social clubs
- Student clubs and organizations
- Watching varsity sports teams
- Meeting new and different people
- Social activities
- Housing and food options
- Participating in varsity sports

Importance to college satisfaction and success

By size of college

	MEANS		
	LARGE COLLEGES	MEDIUM COLLEGES	SMALL COLLEGES
Course content and range of courses	8.7	8.8	9.0
Quality of professors and ability to interact with them	8.4	8.7	9.0
Prospects for job/graduate school	8.4	8.6	8.6
Meeting new and different people	8.1	8.1	8.1
Classrooms, labs, computer facilities	7.9	8.3	8.3
Social activities	7.5	7.6	7.4
Transportation and parking options	7.4	8.0	7.5
Recreational sports and activities	*7.4*	*7.6*	*7.2*
Housing and food options	7.4	7.6	7.4
Beauty of the campus/community	7.4	7.5	7.6
Diversity of student body	7.0	7.6	7.6
Internships	6.9	7.6	7.4
Cultural opportunities	6.9	7.3	7.4
Part-time/full-time job	6.3	7.2	6.7
Stuent clubs and organizations	6.2	6.5	6.3
Study abroad	6.1	6.2	6.5
Shopping, entertainment, restaurants, etc. options	6.0	6.5	6.0
Community service opportunities	5.9	6.1	6.2
Watch varsity sports teams	5.8	6.2	5.7
Sorority/fraternity/social clubs	5.5	5.7	5.5
Participate in varsity sports	5.1	6.0	5.4

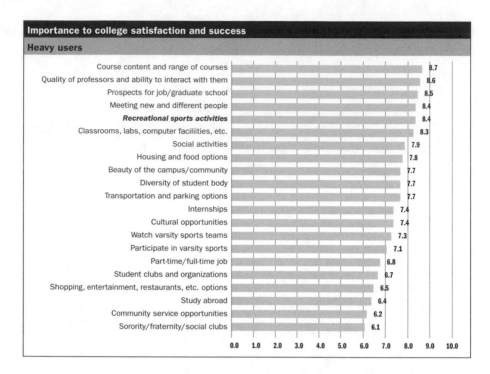

Importance to college satisfaction and success

Heavy users

Course content and range of courses	8.7
Quality of professors and ability to interact with them	8.6
Prospects for job/graduate school	8.5
Meeting new and different people	8.4
Recreational sports activities	8.4
Classrooms, labs, computer faciliities, etc.	8.3
Social activities	7.9
Housing and food options	7.8
Beauty of the campus/community	7.7
Diversity of student body	7.7
Transportation and parking options	7.7
Internships	7.4
Cultural opportunities	7.4
Watch varsity sports teams	7.3
Participate in varsity sports	7.1
Part-time/full-time job	6.8
Student clubs and organizations	6.7
Shopping, entertainment, restaurants, etc. options	6.5
Study abroad	6.4
Community service opportunities	6.2
Sorority/fraternity/social clubs	6.1

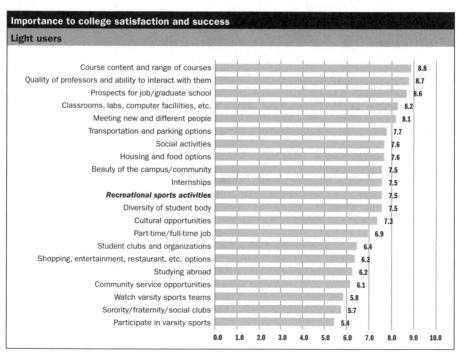

Importance to college satisfaction and success

Light users

Course content and range of courses	8.8
Quality of professors and ability to interact with them	8.7
Prospects for job/graduate school	8.6
Classrooms, labs, computer faciliities, etc.	8.2
Meeting new and different people	8.1
Transportation and parking options	7.7
Social activities	7.6
Housing and food options	7.6
Beauty of the campus/community	7.5
Internships	7.5
Recreational sports activities	7.5
Diversity of student body	7.5
Cultural opportunities	7.3
Part-time/full-time job	6.9
Student clubs and organizations	6.4
Shopping, entertainment, restaurant, etc. options	6.3
Studying abroad	6.2
Community service opportunities	6.1
Watch varsity sports teams	5.8
Sorority/fraternity/social clubs	5.7
Participate in varsity sports	5.4

Importance to college satisfaction and success

Nonusers

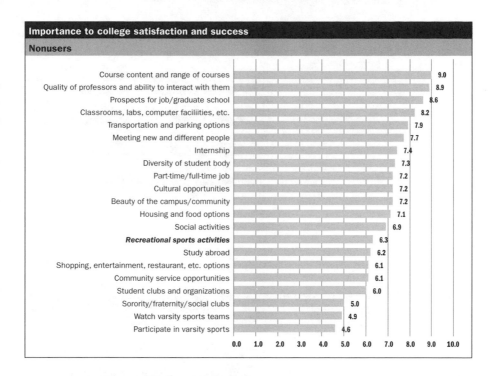

Course content and range of courses	9.0
Quality of professors and ability to interact with them	8.9
Prospects for job/graduate school	8.6
Classrooms, labs, computer faciliities, etc.	8.2
Transportation and parking options	7.9
Meeting new and different people	7.7
Internship	7.4
Diversity of student body	7.3
Part-time/full-time job	7.2
Cultural opportunities	7.2
Beauty of the campus/community	7.2
Housing and food options	7.1
Social activities	6.9
Recreational sports activities	6.3
Study abroad	6.2
Shopping, entertainment, restaurant, etc. options	6.1
Community service opportunities	6.1
Student clubs and organizations	6.0
Sorority/fraternity/social clubs	5.0
Watch varsity sports teams	4.9
Participate in varsity sports	4.6

Importance to college satisfaction and success

Recreational sports rank among 21 factors

	RECREATIONAL SPORTS RANK AMONG 21 FACTORS
All students	11th
By year in school	
Freshman	9th
Sophomore	11th
Junior	10th
Senior	11th
Graduate	10th
By gender	
Male	6th
Female	13th
By ethnicity	
African American	13th
Asian	12th
Caucasian	9th
Hispanic/Latino/Chicano	11th
Other	12th

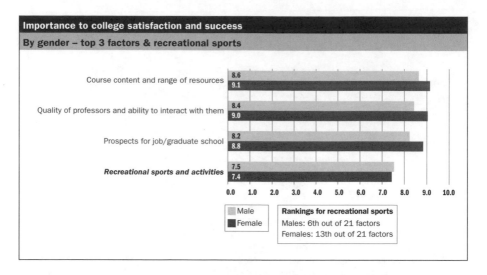

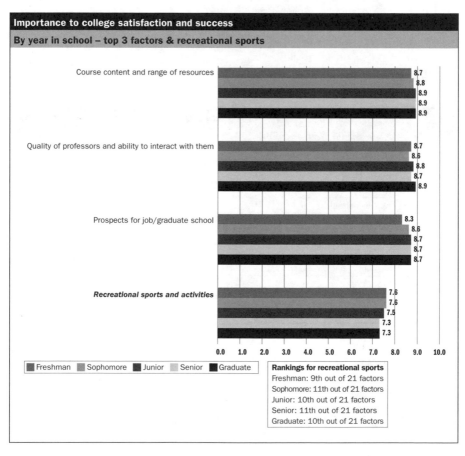

Importance to college satisfaction and success

By ethnicity – top 3 factors & recreational sports

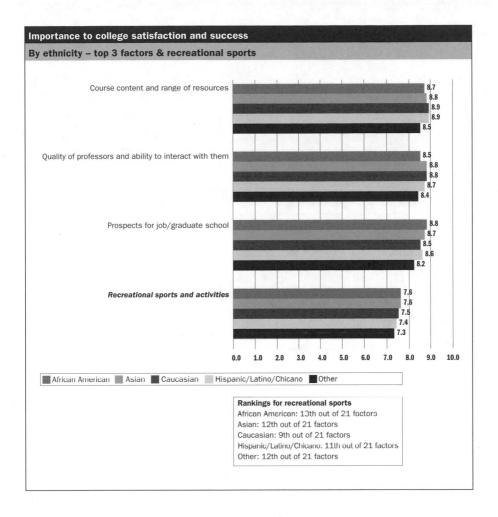

Legend: African American — Asian — Caucasian — Hispanic/Latino/Chicano — Other

Course content and range of resources
8.7
8.8
8.9
8.9
8.5

Quality of professors and ability to interact with them
8.5
8.8
8.8
8.7
8.4

Prospects for job/graduate school
8.8
8.7
8.5
8.6
8.2

Recreational sports and activities
7.6
7.6
7.5
7.4
7.3

0.0 1.0 2.0 3.0 4.0 5.0 6.0 7.0 8.0 9.0 10.0

Rankings for recreational sports
African American: 13th out of 21 factors
Asian: 12th out of 21 factors
Caucasian: 9th out of 21 factors
Hispanic/Latino/Chicano: 11th out of 21 factors
Other: 12th out of 21 factors

Importance to college satisfaction and success		
By type of college		
	MEANS	
	PUBLIC COLLEGES	PRIVATE COLLEGES
Course content and range of courses	8.8	8.9
Quality of professors and ability to interact with them	8.7	8.8
Prospects for job/graduate school	8.5	8.6
Classrooms, labs, computer facilities, etc.	8.2	8.2
Meeting new and different people	8.1	8.1
Transportation and parking options	7.8	7.5
Beauty of the campus/community	7.5	7.7
Housing and food options	7.5	7.6
Recreational sports and activities	*7.5*	*7.4*
Social activities	7.5	4.6
Diversity of student body	7.4	7.7
Internships	7.4	7.6
Cultural opportunities	7.2	7.7
Part-time/full-time job	7.0	6.7
Stuent clubs and organizations	6.4	6.5
Shopping, entertainment, restaurants, etc. options	6.4	6.0
Study abroad	6.2	6.6
Community service opportunities	6.1	6.2
Watch varsity sports teams	6.0	5.8
Participate in varsity sports	5.8	5.4
Sorority/fraternity/social clubs	5.6	5.7

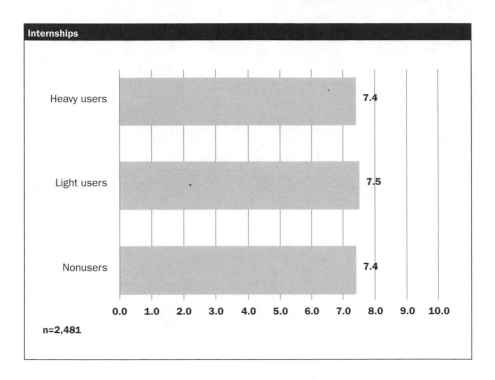

Internships

Heavy users 7.4

Light users 7.5

Nonusers 7.4

0.0 1.0 2.0 3.0 4.0 5.0 6.0 7.0 8.0 9.0 10.0

n=2,481

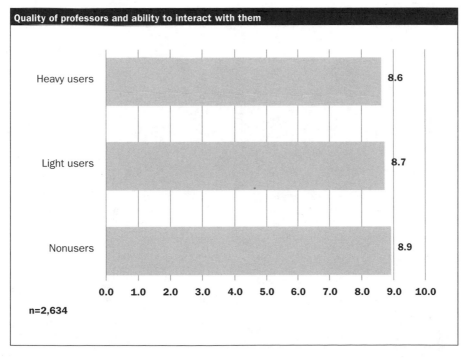

Quality of professors and ability to interact with them

Heavy users 8.6

Light users 8.7

Nonusers 8.9

0.0 1.0 2.0 3.0 4.0 5.0 6.0 7.0 8.0 9.0 10.0

n=2,634

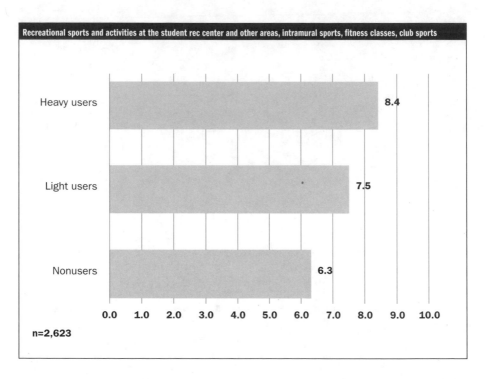

Recreational sports and activities at the student rec center and other areas, intramural sports, fitness classes, club sports

Heavy users — 8.4

Light users — 7.5

Nonusers — 6.3

n=2,623

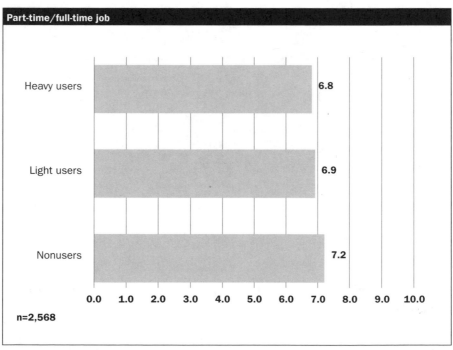

Part-time/full-time job

Heavy users — 6.8

Light users — 6.9

Nonusers — 7.2

n=2,568

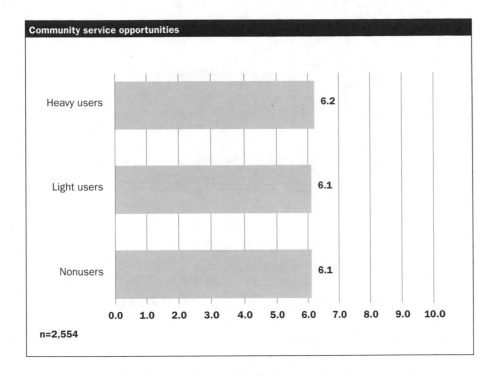

Community service opportunities

Heavy users	6.2
Light users	6.1
Nonusers	6.1

0.0 1.0 2.0 3.0 4.0 5.0 6.0 7.0 8.0 9.0 10.0

n=2,554

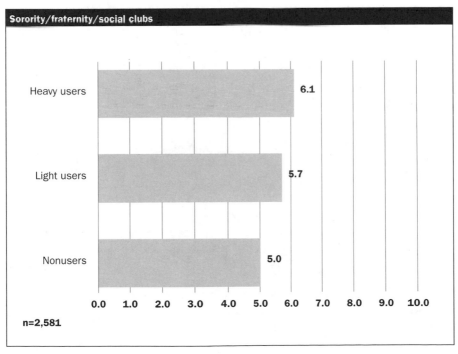

Sorority/fraternity/social clubs

Heavy users	6.1
Light users	5.7
Nonusers	5.0

0.0 1.0 2.0 3.0 4.0 5.0 6.0 7.0 8.0 9.0 10.0

n=2,581

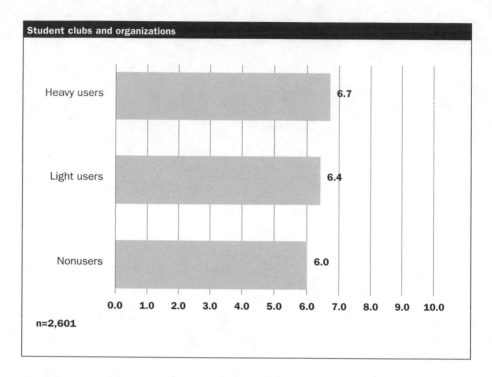

Student clubs and organizations

Heavy users — 6.7

Light users — 6.4

Nonusers — 6.0

n=2,601

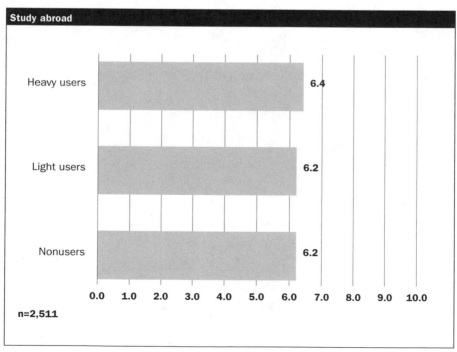

Study abroad

Heavy users — 6.4

Light users — 6.2

Nonusers — 6.2

n=2,511

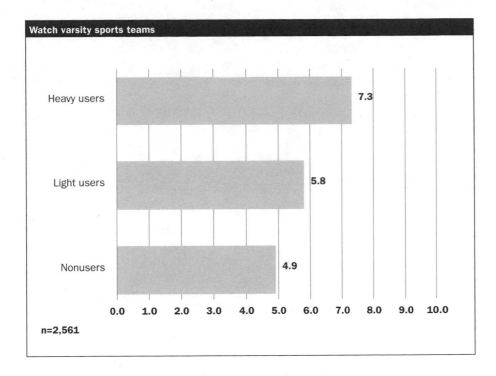

Watch varsity sports teams

Heavy users — 7.3
Light users — 5.8
Nonusers — 4.9

0.0 1.0 2.0 3.0 4.0 5.0 6.0 7.0 8.0 9.0 10.0

n=2,561

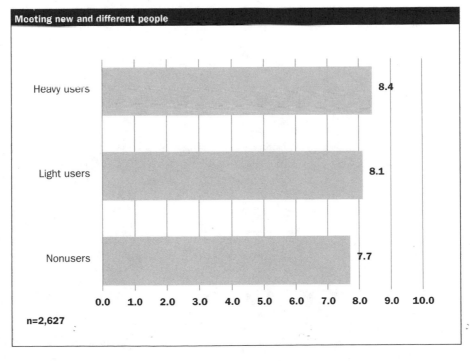

Meeting new and different people

Heavy users — 8.4
Light users — 8.1
Nonusers — 7.7

0.0 1.0 2.0 3.0 4.0 5.0 6.0 7.0 8.0 9.0 10.0

n=2,627

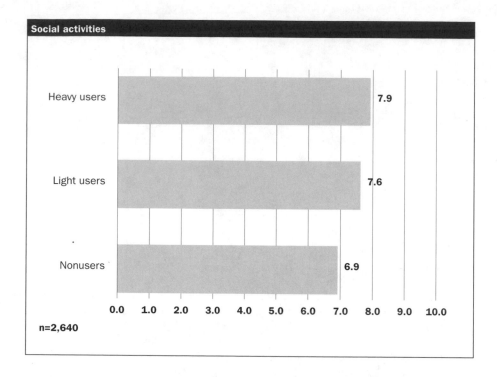

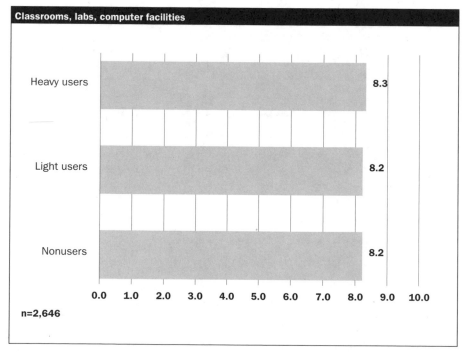

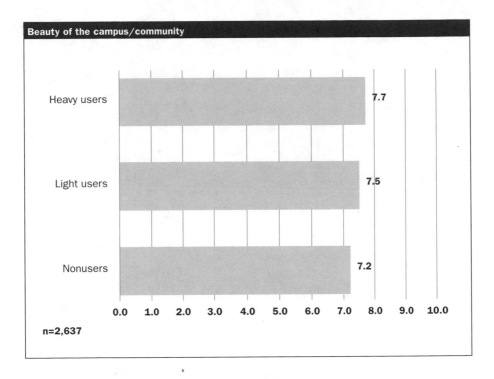

Beauty of the campus/community

Heavy users — 7.7
Light users — 7.5
Nonusers — 7.2

0.0 1.0 2.0 3.0 4.0 5.0 6.0 7.0 8.0 9.0 10.0

n=2,637

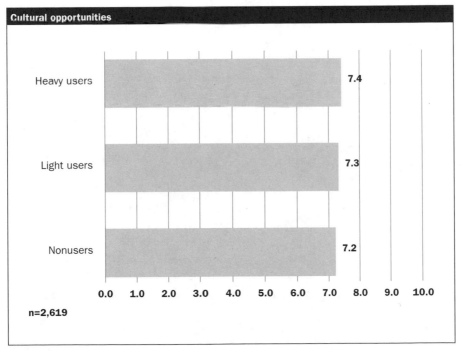

Cultural opportunities

Heavy users — 7.4
Light users — 7.3
Nonusers — 7.2

0.0 1.0 2.0 3.0 4.0 5.0 6.0 7.0 8.0 9.0 10.0

n=2,619

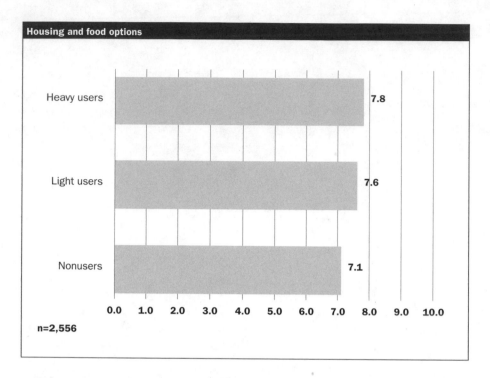

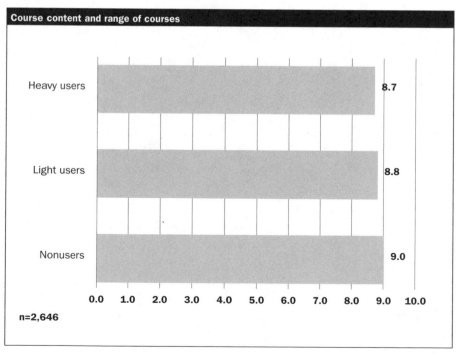

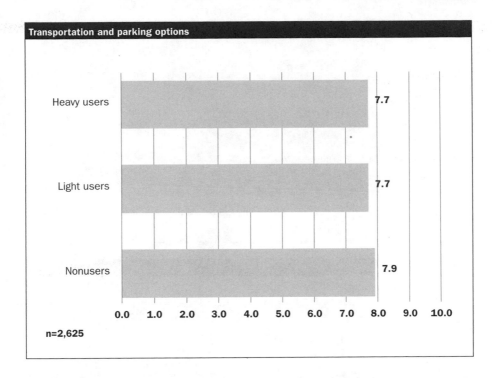

Transportation and parking options

Heavy users — 7.7

Light users — 7.7

Nonusers — 7.9

0.0 1.0 2.0 3.0 4.0 5.0 6.0 7.0 8.0 9.0 10.0

n=2,625

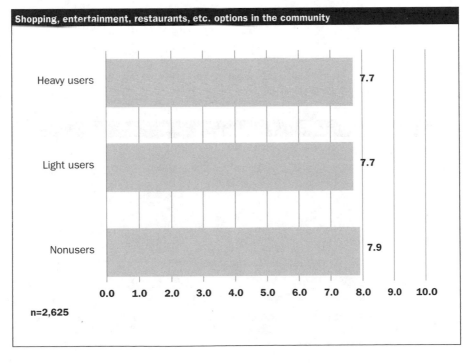

Shopping, entertainment, restaurants, etc. options in the community

Heavy users — 7.7

Light users — 7.7

Nonusers — 7.9

0.0 1.0 2.0 3.0 4.0 5.0 6.0 7.0 8.0 9.0 10.0

n=2,625

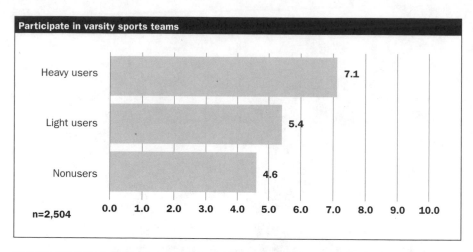

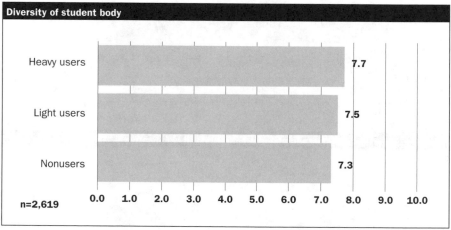

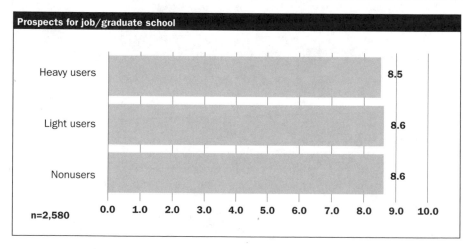

Allocation of Money on Campus

Students were requested to indicate which programs or areas of campus were priorities for receiving more financial resources. Using a 10-point scale where 1 was strongly disagree and 10 was strongly agree, students were asked, "In your opinion, your college should spend more money on…" The following options were offered:

- Classrooms and buildings
- Professors
- Recreational sports activities, student recreation centers and other facilities
- Recruiting students
- Computers, labs, technology, etc.
- Libraries and books
- Campus organizations, clubs and activities
- Varsity athletic programs
- Dormitories and housing
- Landscaping

Average ratings are shown in the graph on the next page. Students selected professors (average rating = 7.9) as the number one priority for more college resources. Computers, labs, technology, etc. (7.8) and libraries and books (7.7) were a close second and third on the students' list for receiving more money. After the top three, there was a considerable drop (7.3) to the fourth spot occupied by dormitories and housing with classrooms and buildings (7.2) close behind. There was another drop in average ratings with recreational sports (6.8) ranked sixth out of ten alternatives. Varsity athletic programs placed last with recruiting students ninth.

Graphs on pages 48-49 show how heavy, light and nonusers of recreational sports programs and activities prioritized areas for receiving more campus money. Heavy users placed computers, labs, technology, etc. first in line for more campus money. Professors were in a virtual tie with computers, labs, technology, etc., and recreational sports programs and activities placed a close third with an average rating of 7.7. While light and nonusers of recreational sports placed professors first, heavy users placed professors second in terms of receiving more money. Other students ranked varsity athletic programs last in terms of receiving additional funding, while heavy users of recreational sports programs placed

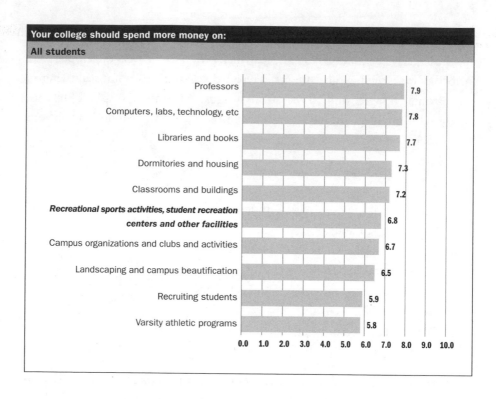

Your college should spend more money on:

All students

Professors	7.9
Computers, labs, technology, etc	7.8
Libraries and books	7.7
Dormitories and housing	7.3
Classrooms and buildings	7.2
Recreational sports activities, student recreation centers and other facilities	6.8
Campus organizations and clubs and activities	6.7
Landscaping and campus beautification	6.5
Recruiting students	5.9
Varsity athletic programs	5.8

0.0 1.0 2.0 3.0 4.0 5.0 6.0 7.0 8.0 9.0 10.0

varsity athletic programs eighth out of ten options. While other students ranked libraries and books higher than recreational sports programs, heavy users ranked libraries and books fifth, two notches below campus recreational sports programs.

The extent to which students believed more money should be spent on campus recreational programs did not vary considerably based on class level, gender or ethnicity. For example, recreational sports programs were ranked sixth for increased expenditures by males and seventh by females. Recreational sports ranked sixth or seventh for all undergraduate class levels and fifth for graduate students. Caucasians and Hispanics ranked recreational sports sixth, while Asians and African Americans ranked it seventh and eighth, respectively.

The graphs on pages 50-52 shows the ratings on a 10-point scale that different segments of students gave to recreational sports in terms of deserving more money. Heavy users assigned recreational sports programs an average score of 7.7, while nonusers gave an average score of only 5.9. Males' average score (6.9) was slightly higher than the one assigned to recreational sports by females (6.7).

Average scores across class levels were stable until the senior year when the scores began to drop. The average scores given to recreational sports were highest for African-Americans and Hispanics, yet scores for Asians and Caucasians were very close.

Public vs. Private Colleges

Students at public colleges (see page 52) ranked recreational sports programs sixth in terms of which areas should receive additional money. Students at private colleges ranked recreational sports seventh.

Size of College

The size of college (see page 52) slightly impacts the extent to which students believed that recreational sports programs were worthy of more money. Recreational Sports programs ranked sixth for students from large and medium sized colleges, and sevenths from small colleges.

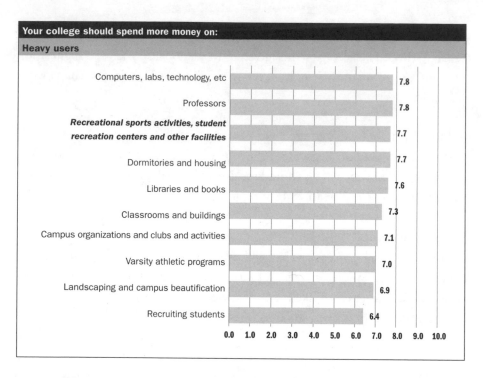

Your college should spend more money on:

Heavy users

Category	Value
Computers, labs, technology, etc	7.8
Professors	7.8
Recreational sports activities, student recreation centers and other facilities	7.7
Dormitories and housing	7.7
Libraries and books	7.6
Classrooms and buildings	7.3
Campus organizations and clubs and activities	7.1
Varsity athletic programs	7.0
Landscaping and campus beautification	6.9
Recruiting students	6.4

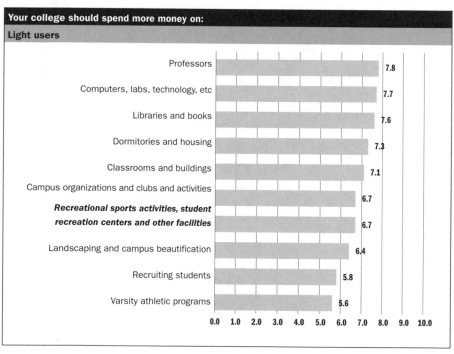

Your college should spend more money on:

Light users

Category	Value
Professors	7.8
Computers, labs, technology, etc	7.7
Libraries and books	7.6
Dormitories and housing	7.3
Classrooms and buildings	7.1
Campus organizations and clubs and activities	6.7
Recreational sports activities, student recreation centers and other facilities	6.7
Landscaping and campus beautification	6.4
Recruiting students	5.8
Varsity athletic programs	5.6

Your college should spend more money on:

Nonusers

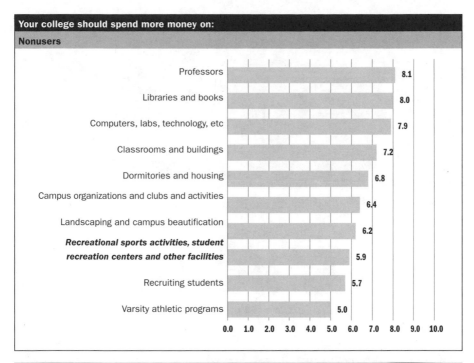

Your college should spend more money on:

Recreational sports rank among 10 factors

	RECREATIONAL SPORTS RANK AMONG 21 FACTORS
All students	6th
By year in school	
Freshman	7th
Sophomore	7th
Junior	7th
Senior	6th
Graduate	5th
By gender	
Male	6th
Female	7th
By ethnicity	
African American	8th
Asian	7th
Caucasian	6th
Hispanic/Latino/Chicano	6th
Other	7th

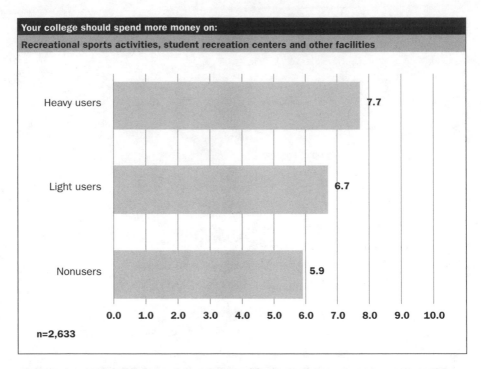

Your college should spend more money on:

Recreational sports activities, student recreation centers and other facilities

Heavy users — 7.7
Light users — 6.7
Nonusers — 5.9

n=2,633

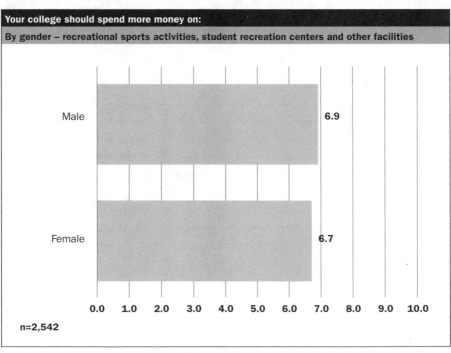

Your college should spend more money on:

By gender – recreational sports activities, student recreation centers and other facilities

Male — 6.9
Female — 6.7

n=2,542

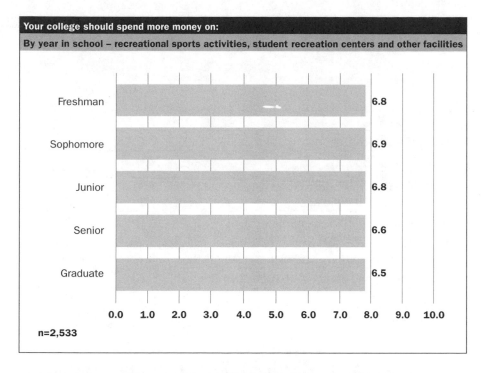

Your college should spend more money on:

By year in school – recreational sports activities, student recreation centers and other facilities

Freshman	6.8
Sophomore	6.9
Junior	6.8
Senior	6.6
Graduate	6.5

0.0 1.0 2.0 3.0 4.0 5.0 6.0 7.0 8.0 9.0 10.0

n=2,533

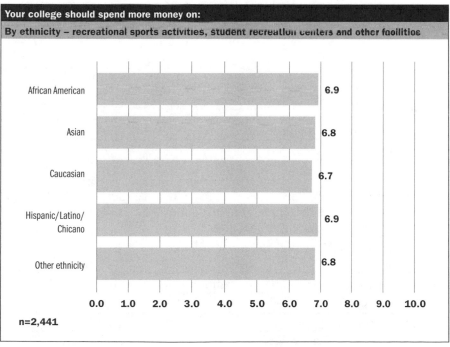

Your college should spend more money on:

By ethnicity – recreational sports activities, student recreation centers and other facilities

African American	6.9
Asian	6.8
Caucasian	6.7
Hispanic/Latino/Chicano	6.9
Other ethnicity	6.8

0.0 1.0 2.0 3.0 4.0 5.0 6.0 7.0 8.0 9.0 10.0

n=2,441

Your college should spend more money on:

By type of college

	MEANS	
	PUBLIC COLLEGES	PRIVATE COLLEGES
Professors	7.9	7.9
Computers, labs, technology, etc.	7.8	7.7
Libraries and books	7.6	7.8
Dormitories and housing	7.2	7.4
Classrooms and buildings	7.2	7.0
Recreational sports activities, student recreation centers and other facilities	6.8	6.7
Campus organizations and clubs and activities	6.7	6.8
Landscaping and campus beautification	6.5	6.4
Recruiting students	5.9	6.0
Varsity athletic programs	5.9	5.5

Importance to college satisfaction and success

By size of college

	MEANS		
	LARGE COLLEGES	MEDIUM COLLEGES	SMALL COLLEGES
Professors	7.5	7.8	8.2
Computers, labs, technology, etc.	7.2	7.9	7.8
Libraries and books	7.2	7.7	7.8
Dormitories and housing	7.0	7.5	7.0
Classrooms and buildings	6.9	7.3	7.0
Recreational sports activities, student recreation centers and other facilities	6.6	6.9	6.5
Campus organizations and clubs and activities	6.5	6.8	6.7
Landscaping and campus beautification	6.4	6.5	6.5
Recruiting students	5.3	6.1	5.9
Varsity athletic programs	5.2	6.1	5.6

Happiness with College Experience

Diener* developed a five-item scale to measure happiness with life. This scale was adapted to a college environment and administered as part of the total questionnaire completed by students on the 16 campuses in the study. Each item was scored on a 10-point scale with 1 being strongly disagreed and 10 being strongly agree. The total scores across the five scale items were summed and divided by five to produce an average score across the five items.

The graph below shows the average happiness scores for heavy, light and nonusers of campus recreational sports programs. Heavy users were slightly happier than light users who were significantly happier than nonusers were. That is, there was a direct and significant correlation between level of participation in campus recreational sports programs and happiness with the college experience.

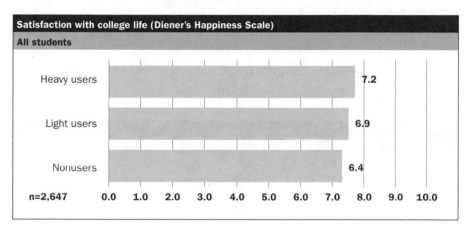

The direct correlation between participation in campus recreational sports programs and happiness with college held for students across all class levels except the junior year. For example, freshmen who were heavy users of campus recreational programs had an average happiness score of 7.2, while nonusers had an average score of 6.3. This same strong relationship held for sophomores, yet there was less of an effect for juniors. Juniors who were either heavy or light users of campus recreational sports programs had virtually the same happiness scores, however, both scores were considerably higher than the happiness score for nonusers. The relationship between participation in campus recreational

*Diener, E., Emmons, R.A., Larsen, R.J. & Griffin, S. (1985). The Satisfaction With Life Scale. *Journal of Personality Assessment, 49*, 71-75.

sports programs and happiness with college life was strong again for seniors and graduate students.

Graphs on pages 54-61 show that heavy users of recreational sports programs were happier with their college life and experiences than light and nonusers regardless of gender or race/ethnic background. For example, male heavy users of recreational sports programs had a happiness score of 7.2 on a 10-point scale, while light users had a score of 6.7 and nonusers had a score of 6.4. This relationship held for females and all ethnic groups except Asians for whom light users were happier than heavy users (both were happier than non users).

Public vs. Private Colleges

Students at private colleges (page 60) (average score of 7.1) were happier than students at public colleges (average score 6.8).

Size of College

Students at larger schools were happiest (average score of 7.1), while students at medium and small schools were virtually equally happy (page 60).

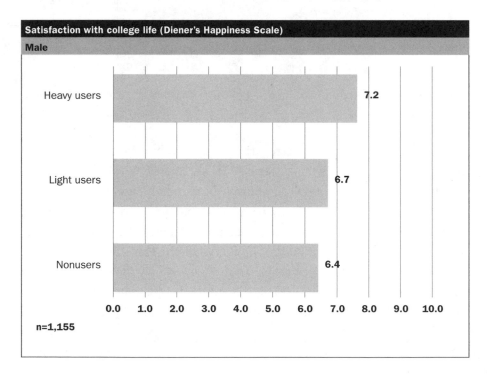

Satisfaction with college life (Diener's Happiness Scale)

Male

- Heavy users: 7.2
- Light users: 6.7
- Nonusers: 6.4

0.0 1.0 2.0 3.0 4.0 5.0 6.0 7.0 8.0 9.0 10.0

n=1,155

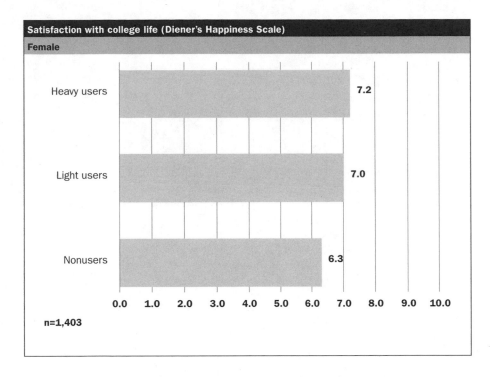

Satisfaction with college life (Diener's Happiness Scale)

Female

Heavy users 7.2
Light users 7.0
Nonusers 6.3

n=1,403

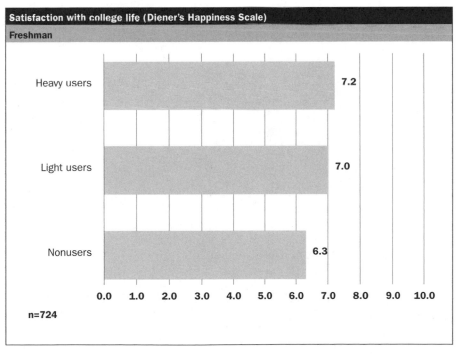

Satisfaction with college life (Diener's Happiness Scale)

Freshman

Heavy users 7.2
Light users 7.0
Nonusers 6.3

n=724

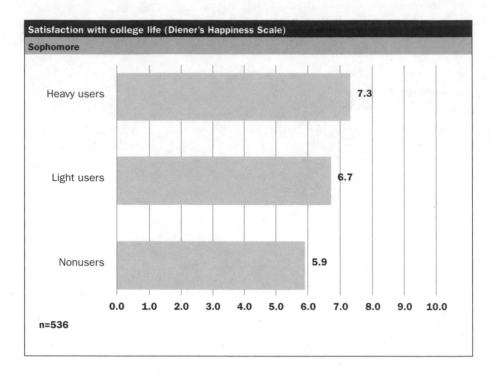

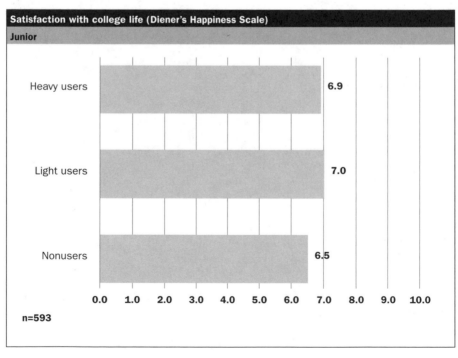

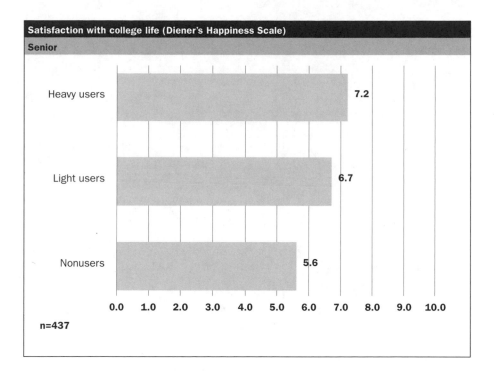

Satisfaction with college life (Diener's Happiness Scale)

Senior

Heavy users — 7.2
Light users — 6.7
Nonusers — 5.6

0.0 1.0 2.0 3.0 4.0 5.0 6.0 7.0 8.0 9.0 10.0

n=437

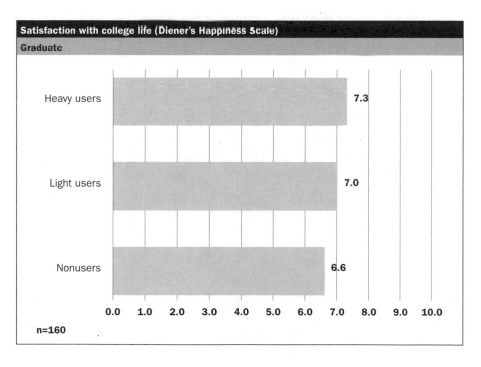

Satisfaction with college life (Diener's Happiness Scale)

Graduate

Heavy users — 7.3
Light users — 7.0
Nonusers — 6.6

0.0 1.0 2.0 3.0 4.0 5.0 6.0 7.0 8.0 9.0 10.0

n=160

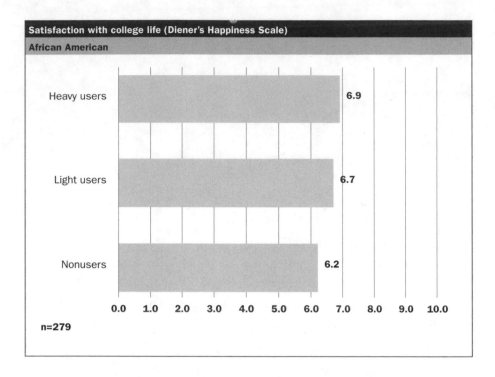

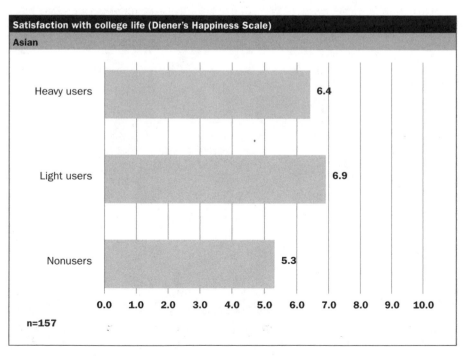

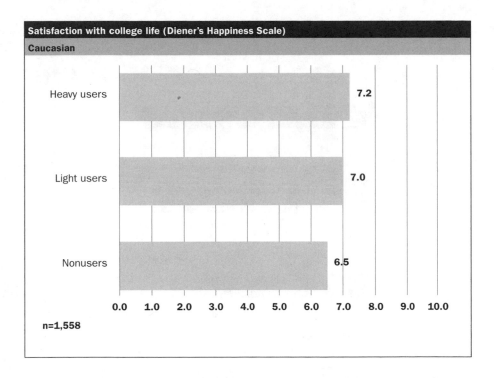

Satisfaction with college life (Diener's Happiness Scale)
Caucasian

Heavy users — 7.2
Light users — 7.0
Nonusers — 6.5

n=1,558

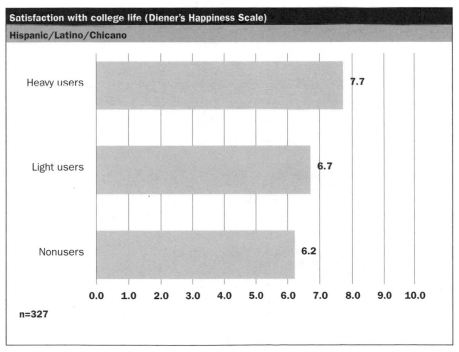

Satisfaction with college life (Diener's Happiness Scale)
Hispanic/Latino/Chicano

Heavy users — 7.7
Light users — 6.7
Nonusers — 6.2

n=327

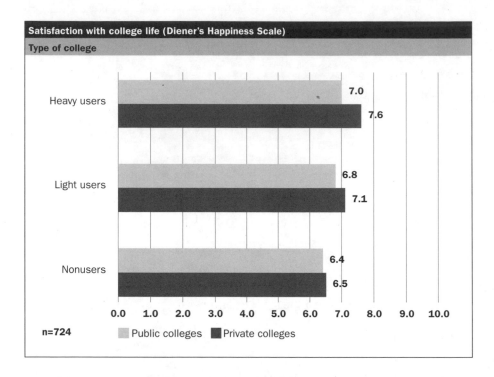

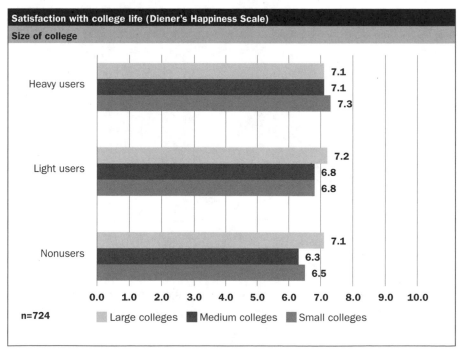

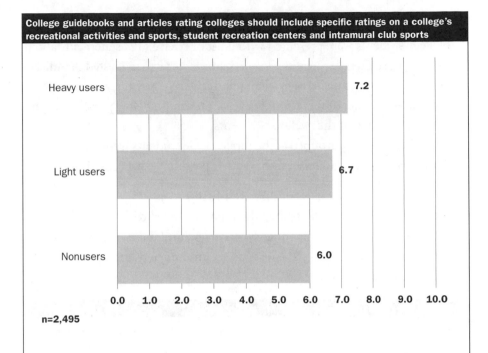

College guidebooks and articles rating colleges should include specific ratings on a college's recreational activities and sports, student recreation centers and intramural club sports

Heavy users — 7.2

Light users — 6.7

Nonusers — 6.0

0.0 1.0 2.0 3.0 4.0 5.0 6.0 7.0 8.0 9.0 10.0

n=2,495

Using a 10-point scale (1 = strongly disagree; 10 = strongly agree), students agreed (even non-users of recreational sports programs) that college guidebooks and articles rating colleges should include more specific information about colleges' recreational and sports programs and activities. As expected, heavy users were more likely to agree.

Benefits of Recreational Sports

College students were presented with a list of twelve (12) statements about the potential benefits of recreational sports. Students were requested to indicate their level of agreement with each statement using a 10-point scale where 1 was strongly disagree, and 10 was strongly agree. The graph below presents the average scores for each of the twelve statements.

Three benefits were grouped at the top: College students were most likely to agree that participation in recreational sports programs and activities:

1. Improves their overall emotional well-being
2. Reduces their stress and helped them handle their workload at college
3. Improves their overall happiness. Closely behind these three benefits was the belief that recreational sports programs and activities improved students' self-confidence

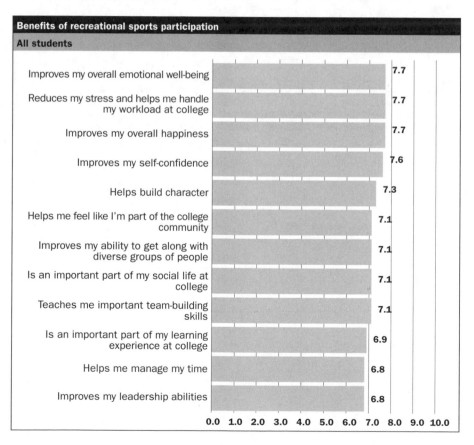

Benefits of recreational sports participation

All students

Statement	Score
Improves my overall emotional well-being	7.7
Reduces my stress and helps me handle my workload at college	7.7
Improves my overall happiness	7.7
Improves my self-confidence	7.6
Helps build character	7.3
Helps me feel like I'm part of the college community	7.1
Improves my ability to get along with diverse groups of people	7.1
Is an important part of my social life at college	7.1
Teaches me important team-building skills	7.1
Is an important part of my learning experience at college	6.9
Helps me manage my time	6.8
Improves my leadership abilities	6.8

Participation in recreational sports programs and activities had more benefit on factors that have a salutary impact on students' overall lives rather than on specific facets of their lives. For example, students were more likely to agree that participation in recreational sports improved emotional well-being, reduced stress, improved happiness and self-confidence and helped build character than to agree that participation helped teach team-building skills, or time management or leadership abilities.

It should be noted that average scores for the twelve (12) benefits were rather tightly grouped, ranging from 7.7 to 6.8. It should also be noted that all average scores were considerably above the midpoint (5.5) of a 1 to 10 scale. That is, there is general agreement that all attributes presented to students in the study were considered benefits of participating in recreational sports programs and activities.

Graphs beginning on this page through page 69 show the extent to which heavy, light and nonusers of campus recreational sports programs and activities agreed that attributes were benefits of participation in recreational sports. As expected, heavy users were more likely than light or nonusers to agree that all attributes were benefits of participation in recreational sports programs. For example, average scores to reflect the degree that participation in recreational sports improved students' overall emotional well-being were as follows:

8.4 Heavy users
7.8 Light users
6.6 Nonusers

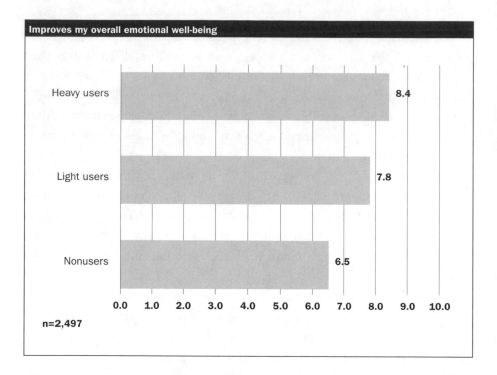

Improves my overall emotional well-being

Heavy users — 8.4
Light users — 7.8
Nonusers — 6.5

0.0 1.0 2.0 3.0 4.0 5.0 6.0 7.0 8.0 9.0 10.0

n=2,497

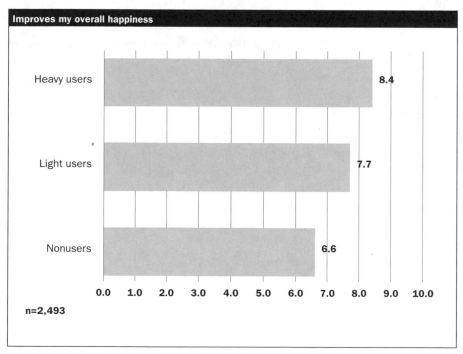

Improves my overall happiness

Heavy users — 8.4
Light users — 7.7
Nonusers — 6.6

0.0 1.0 2.0 3.0 4.0 5.0 6.0 7.0 8.0 9.0 10.0

n=2,493

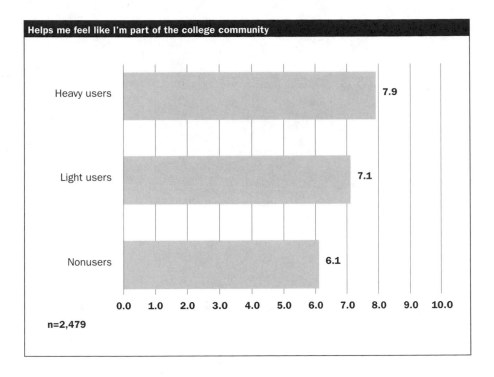

Helps me feel like I'm part of the college community

Heavy users — 7.9
Light users — 7.1
Nonusers — 6.1

0.0 1.0 2.0 3.0 4.0 5.0 6.0 7.0 8.0 9.0 10.0

n=2,479

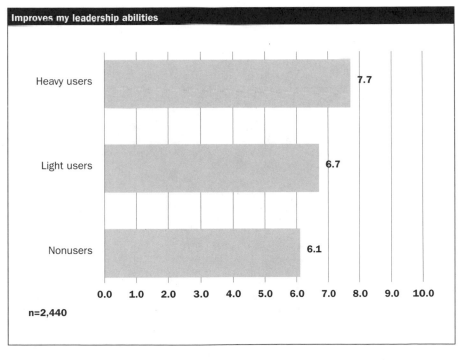

Improves my leadership abilities

Heavy users — 7.7
Light users — 6.7
Nonusers — 6.1

0.0 1.0 2.0 3.0 4.0 5.0 6.0 7.0 8.0 9.0 10.0

n=2,440

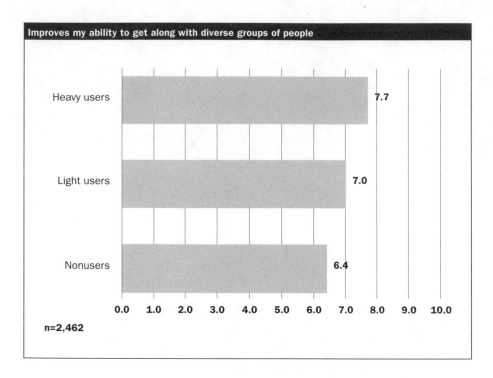

Improves my ability to get along with diverse groups of people

Heavy users — 7.7
Light users — 7.0
Nonusers — 6.4

0.0 1.0 2.0 3.0 4.0 5.0 6.0 7.0 8.0 9.0 10.0

n=2,462

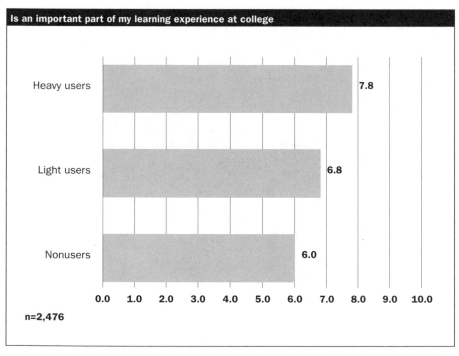

Is an important part of my learning experience at college

Heavy users — 7.8
Light users — 6.8
Nonusers — 6.0

0.0 1.0 2.0 3.0 4.0 5.0 6.0 7.0 8.0 9.0 10.0

n=2,476

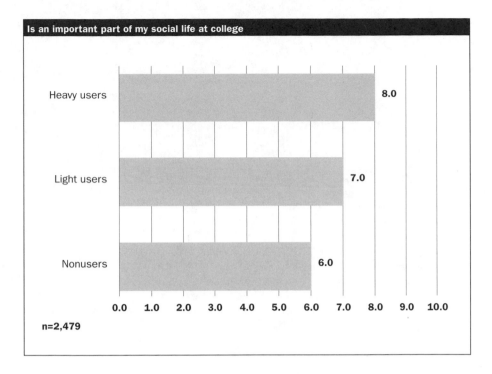

Is an important part of my social life at college

Heavy users — 8.0
Light users — 7.0
Nonusers — 6.0

0.0 1.0 2.0 3.0 4.0 5.0 6.0 7.0 8.0 9.0 10.0

n=2,479

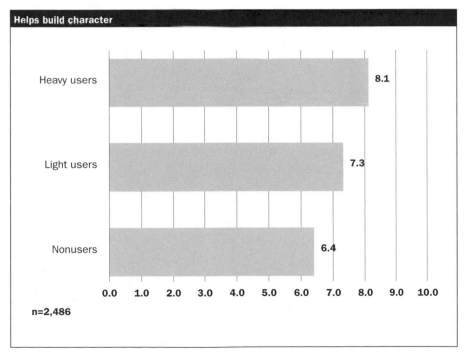

Helps build character

Heavy users — 8.1
Light users — 7.3
Nonusers — 6.4

0.0 1.0 2.0 3.0 4.0 5.0 6.0 7.0 8.0 9.0 10.0

n=2,486

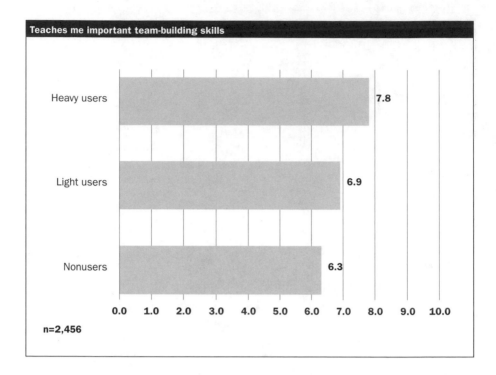

Teaches me important team-building skills

Heavy users	7.8
Light users	6.9
Nonusers	6.3

0.0 1.0 2.0 3.0 4.0 5.0 6.0 7.0 8.0 9.0 10.0

n=2,456

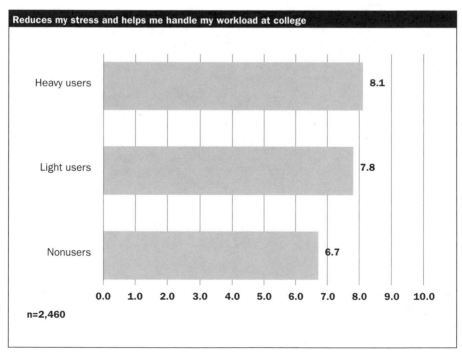

Reduces my stress and helps me handle my workload at college

Heavy users	8.1
Light users	7.8
Nonusers	6.7

0.0 1.0 2.0 3.0 4.0 5.0 6.0 7.0 8.0 9.0 10.0

n=2,460

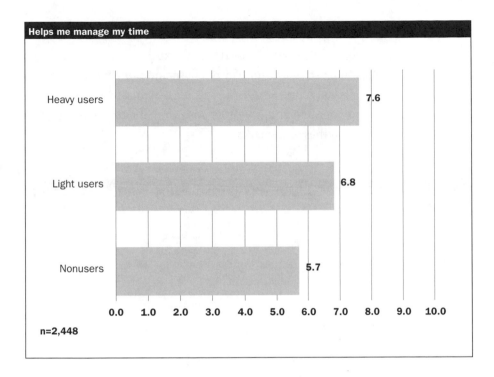

Helps me manage my time

Heavy users 7.6

Light users 6.8

Nonusers 5.7

0.0 1.0 2.0 3.0 4.0 5.0 6.0 7.0 8.0 9.0 10.0

n=2,448

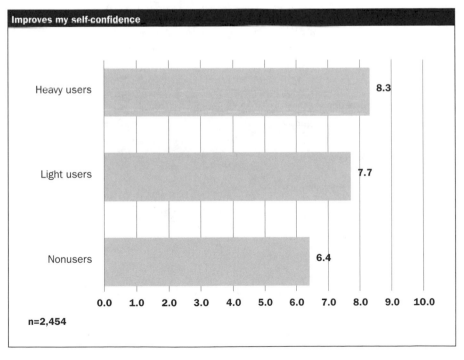

Improves my self-confidence

Heavy users 8.3

Light users 7.7

Nonusers 6.4

0.0 1.0 2.0 3.0 4.0 5.0 6.0 7.0 8.0 9.0 10.0

n=2,454

This direct relationship between the perceived value of recreational sports participation and frequency of participation held for all 12 benefits. Graphs on pages 70 and 71 show the extent to which heavy, light and nonusers agreed that participation in recreational sports resulted in specific benefits. In all cases, heavy users perceived the most benefit and nonusers perceived the least with light users' responses in between these two groups.

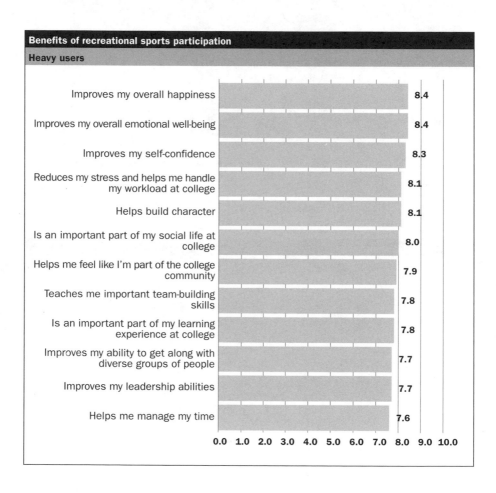

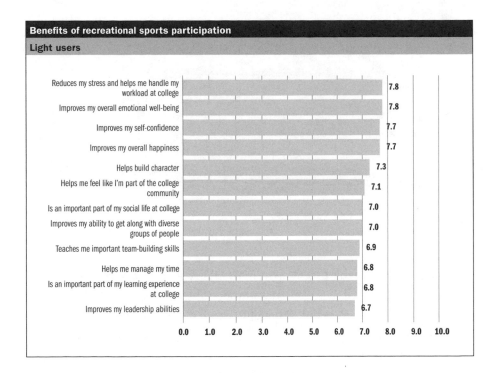

Benefits of recreational sports participation

Light users

Benefit	Value
Reduces my stress and helps me handle my workload at college	7.8
Improves my overall emotional well-being	7.8
Improves my self-confidence	7.7
Improves my overall happiness	7.7
Helps build character	7.3
Helps me feel like I'm part of the college community	7.1
Is an important part of my social life at college	7.0
Improves my ability to get along with diverse groups of people	7.0
Teaches me important team-building skills	6.9
Helps me manage my time	6.8
Is an important part of my learning experience at college	6.8
Improves my leadership abilities	6.7

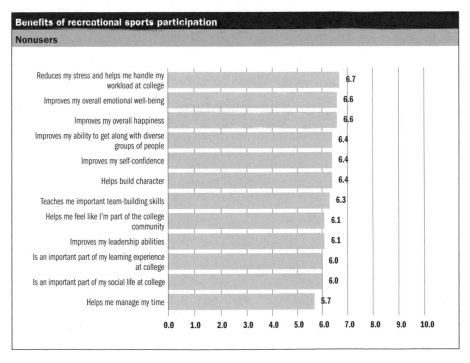

Benefits of recreational sports participation

Nonusers

Benefit	Value
Reduces my stress and helps me handle my workload at college	6.7
Improves my overall emotional well-being	6.6
Improves my overall happiness	6.6
Improves my ability to get along with diverse groups of people	6.4
Improves my self-confidence	6.4
Helps build character	6.4
Teaches me important team-building skills	6.3
Helps me feel like I'm part of the college community	6.1
Improves my leadership abilities	6.1
Is an important part of my learning experience at college	6.0
Is an important part of my social life at college	6.0
Helps me manage my time	5.7

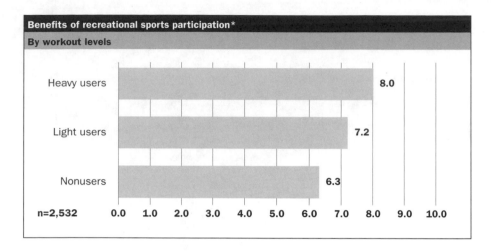

The top graph on this page shows the average score of each attribute summed across the twelve attributes displayed in the graphs on pages 49 and 50. Heavy users average score across the 12 benefits was 8.0 and was significantly higher than the average for light users (7.2), which was significantly higher than the score for nonusers (6.3).

The graph below show average agreement levels across all 12 benefits of recreational sports participation. The value of recreational sports changed little throughout college. Freshmen, sophomores and juniors perceived identical levels of value from participation in recreational sports. The value of recreational sports programs and activities declined slightly for seniors and graduate students.

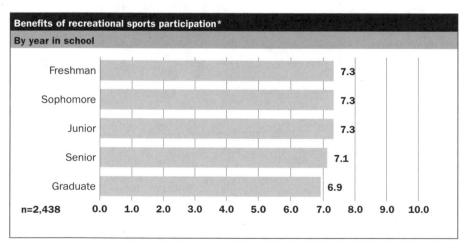

*Average score across 12 questions concerning beneficial outcomes of recreational sports.

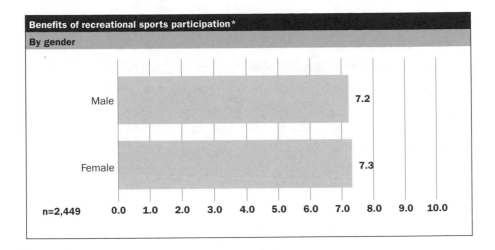

As shown by the graph on the top of this page, males and females perceived the benefits of participation in recreational sports programs and activities nearly identically. Females were slightly more likely to agree with the series of 12 statements that described the benefits of participating in recreational sports programs and activities.

African Americans were slightly more likely to agree with the statements about benefits of recreational sports than students of other races/ethnic backgrounds were. The graph below shows that Asians were least likely to agree with the statements enumerating the benefits of recreational sports, while African Americans were slightly more likely to agree than Caucasians and Hispanics.

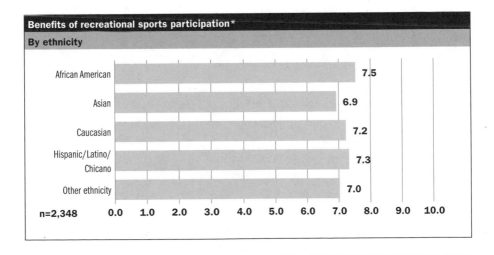

*Average score across 12 questions concerning beneficial outcomes of recreational sports.

Public vs. Private Colleges

There were slight differences in levels of agreement with the benefits statements about recreational sports between students at public colleges and students at private colleges (below). However, none of the differences exceeded 0.2 on a 10-point scale. For example, public college students had an average of 7.7 when assessing recreational sports contribution to higher self confidence. Students at private colleges had a score of 7.5.

Size of College

The table on page 75 shows the average scores reflecting the benefits of recreational sports to students at large, medium and small colleges. In general, students at medium sized colleges were slightly more likely to agree with the benefit statements about recreational sports programs. Another way of interpreting this result is to say that students at medium size colleges were slightly more likely to

Benefits of recreational sports participation		
By type of college		
	MEANS	
	PUBLIC COLLEGES	PRIVATE COLLEGES
Improves my overall emotional well-being	7.7	7.7
Improves my overall happiness	7.7	7.7
Reduces my stress and helps me handle my workload at college	7.7	7.6
Improves my self-confidence	7.7	7.5
Helps build character	7.4	7.3
Helps me feel like I'm part of the college community	7.1	7.3
Is an important part of my social life at college	7.1	7.1
Improves my ability to get along with diverse groups of people	7.1	6.9
Teaches me important team-building skills	7.0	7.1
Is an important part of my learning experience at college	6.9	6.9
Helps me manage my time	6.9	6.7
Improves my leadership abilities	6.8	6.9

perceive the benefits of participation in recreational sports programs and activities.

There were some significant differences in levels of agreement to benefit statements by students from different size colleges. For example, students at large colleges were more likely to agree that participation in recreational sports reduced their stress and helped them handle their workload at college. Students at medium and small colleges were more likely to agree that participation in recreational sports programs and activities improved their leadership abilities.

Benefits of recreational sports participation			
By size of college			
	MEANS		
	LARGE COLLEGES	MEDIUM COLLEGES	SMALL COLLEGES
Reduces my stress and helps me handle my workload at college	8.1	7.7	7.5
Improves my overall emotional well-being	7.9	7.7	7.6
Improves my overall happiness	7.9	7.7	7.6
Improves my self-confidence	7.7	7.7	7.4
Helps build character	7.2	7.4	7.2
Helps me manage my time	7.0	6.9	6.5
Helps me feel like I'm part of the college community	6.8	7.2	7.1
Improves my ability to get along with diverse groups of people	6.8	7.2	7.0
Is an important part of my social life at college	6.7	7.2	6.9
Teaches me important team-building skills	6.7	7.1	7.1
Is an important part of my learning experience at college	6.6	7.0	6.8
Improves my leadership abilities	6.4	6.9	6.9

Selected Behaviors and Recreational Sports Participation

This section of the report examines the relationship between participation in recreational sports programs and activities and selected behaviors. Some behaviors were positive such as participating in community service, while other behaviors were negative such as using illegal drugs.

The graph on top of page 77 summarizes the number of times in the past 30 days students engaged in certain behaviors. Students, on average consumed more than three alcoholic drinks at a sitting 3.8 times. That is, nearly four times a month, the typical college student drank heavily. One out-of-two students (51%) consumed more than three drinks in a given day at least once in the past month.

The typical college student also smoked three days a month, used illegal drugs nearly twice a month, and attended religious services twice a month. One out-of-five college students smoked (22%); 17 percent used illegal drugs in the past month, and 37 percent had attended religious services in the preceding month.

Students, on average, missed about one and a half days of school or work because of illness, about a third of this missed time (1.4 days/0.4 days = .37 days), was due to over consumption of alcohol or illegal drugs. Two out of five students

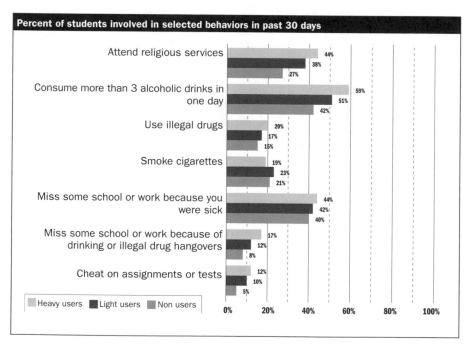

Percent of students involved in selected behaviors in past 30 days

Attend religious services — 44%, 38%, 27%
Consume more than 3 alcoholic drinks in one day — 59%, 51%, 42%
Use illegal drugs — 20%, 17%, 15%
Smoke cigarettes — 19%, 23%, 21%
Miss some school or work because you were sick — 44%, 42%, 40%
Miss some school or work because of drinking or illegal drug hangovers — 17%, 12%, 8%
Cheat on assignments or tests — 12%, 10%, 5%

Heavy users   Light users   Non users

0%   20%   40%   60%   80%   100%

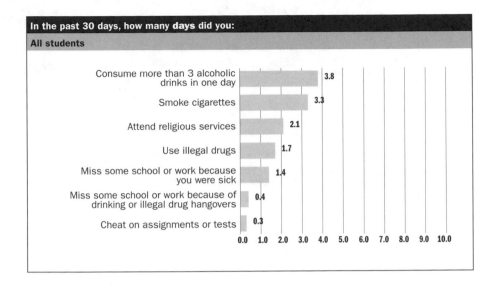

In the past 30 days, how many **days** did you:

All students

(42%) missed some work or school time because of illness; 12 percent because of illness related to alcohol or illegal drug consumption. Finally, there was little cheating on tests or assignments as the typical college student cheated 0.3 times per month; in all, 9 percent of college students reported cheating on an assignment or test in the past month.

Graphs on pages 77 and 78 show behavioral statistics for heavy, light and nonusers of campus recreational sports programs and activities.

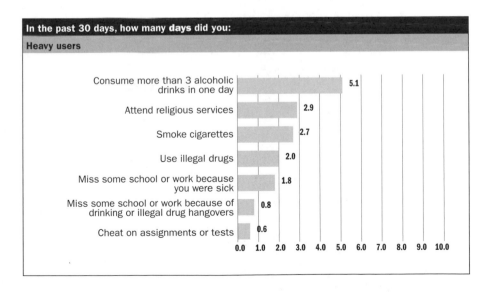

In the past 30 days, how many **days** did you:

Heavy users

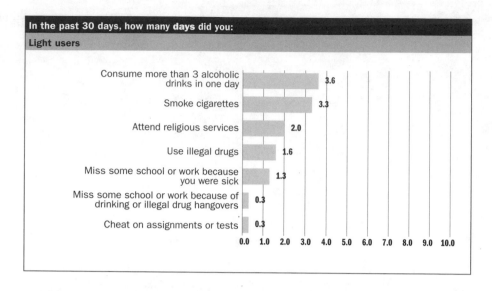

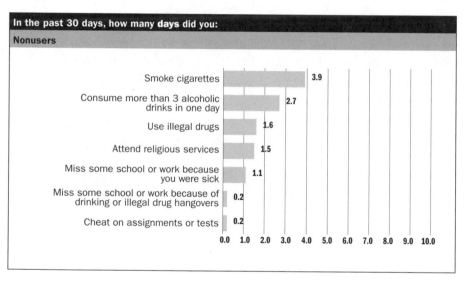

The graph on page 79 shows that participation in religious services and participation in recreational sports activities were directly correlated. That is, heavy users of recreational sports activities were more likely to attend religious services.

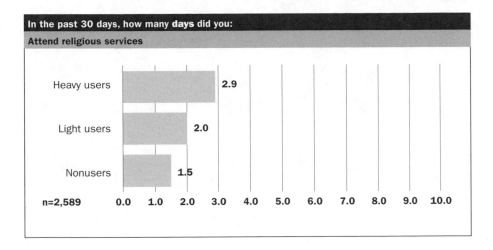

Participation in recreational sports was directly correlated to community service. On average, heavy users of recreational sports committed 7.4 hours a month to community service compared to only 5.1 hours for nonusers.

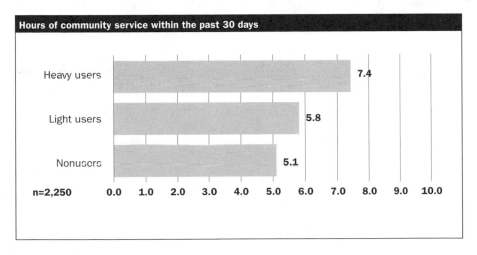

However, the picture painted by the graphs beginning on page 80 thorugh 82 are less flattering of recreational sports participants. Heavy users of recreational sports consumed at least three alcoholic drinks a day more often than light or nonusers. This same type of relationship existed between participation in recreational sports and illegal drug use, cheating in school, missing days of work or school and missing days of work or school because of consumption of alcohol or illegal drugs.

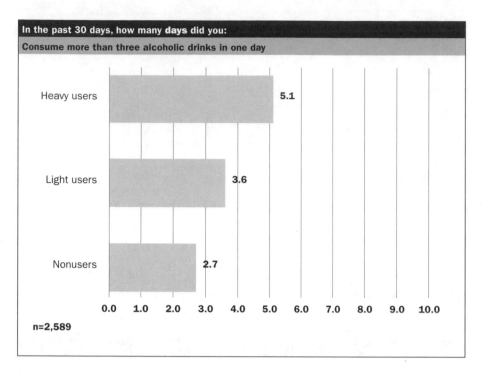

In the past 30 days, how many days did you:

Consume more than three alcoholic drinks in one day

Heavy users — 5.1

Light users — 3.6

Nonusers — 2.7

n=2,589

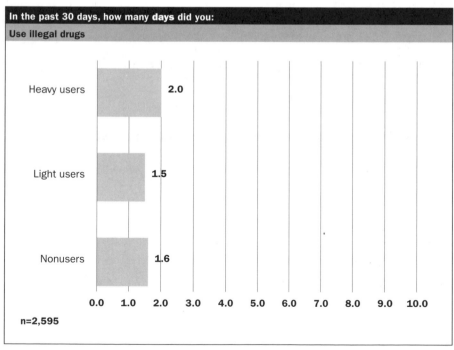

In the past 30 days, how many days did you:

Use illegal drugs

Heavy users — 2.0

Light users — 1.5

Nonusers — 1.6

n=2,595

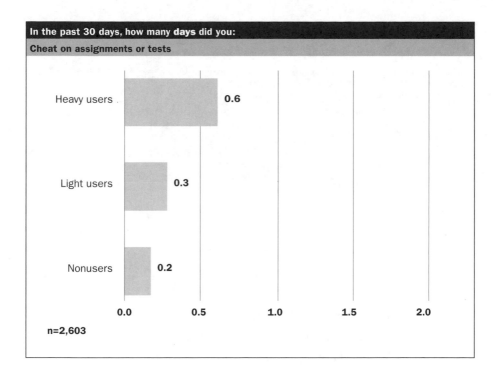

In the past 30 days, how many **days** did you:

Cheat on assignments or tests

Heavy users — 0.6

Light users — 0.3

Nonusers — 0.2

0.0   0.5   1.0   1.5   2.0

n=2,603

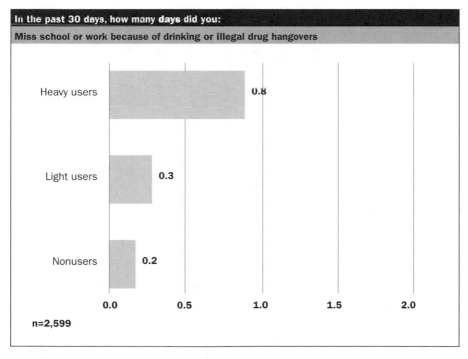

In the past 30 days, how many **days** did you:

Miss school or work because of drinking or illegal drug hangovers

Heavy users — 0.8

Light users — 0.3

Nonusers — 0.2

0.0   0.5   1.0   1.5   2.0

n=2,599

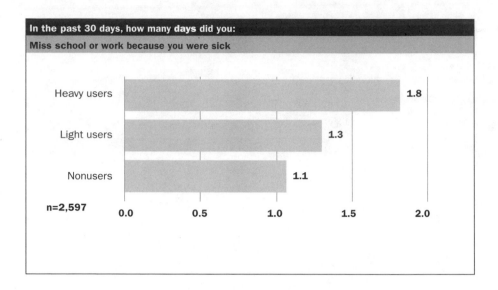

However, there was an inverse relationship between participation in recreational sports and smoking. Students who participated frequently in recreational sports smoked least and nonparticipants smoked most.

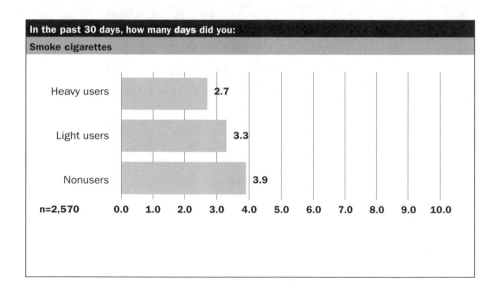

Heavy users of recreational sports worked, on average, four fewer hours a week in outside jobs compared to nonusers. Light users worked essentially the same number of hours a week as heavy users. Nearly two out-of-three heavy users (65%) worked in outside jobs compared, to 66 percent of light and 72 percent of nonusers.

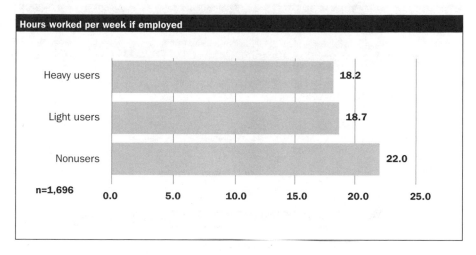

Heavy users of recreational sports took more academic credit hours per term than nonusers did with the difference being nearly one credit hour. This difference translates to eight credit hours (for colleges using semesters) over a four-year period, or over half the hours that students normally take in a term.

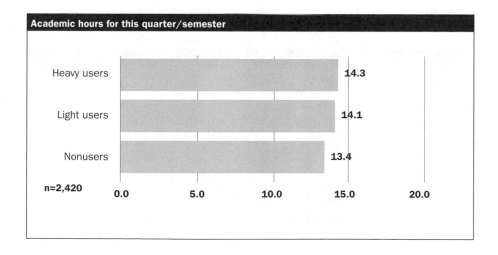

The SAT and ACT Assessment scores were not significantly correlated with recreational sports activities. Heavy and light users of recreational sports had slightly higher SAT scores, yet scores on the ACT were virtually identical across groups. Grade point averages (GPA) were also nearly identical across usage groups.

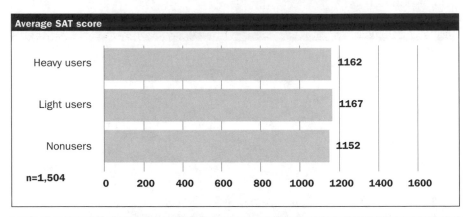

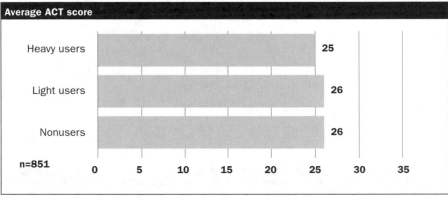

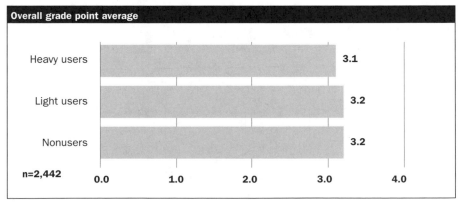

There was basically no difference in the percentage of college expenses paid by students based on their participation level in recreational sports. All three groups of students paid about one-fifth of their college expenses.

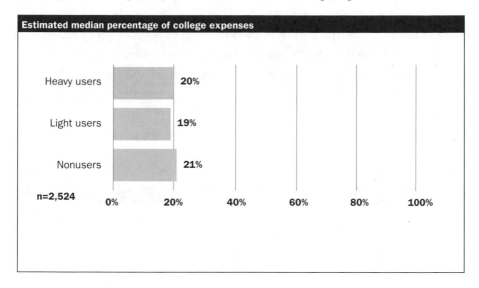

Usage of college recreational facilities was directly correlated to how far students lived from the recreation center. Heavy users lived an average of 5.6 miles from the recreation center, while nonusers lived over ten miles away.

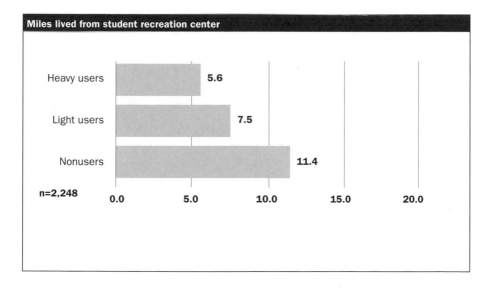

Profile

This section of the report presents profile information for the students in the study. A wide range of academic majors was represented in the study, headed by business, liberal arts and social sciences. Participants in the study were rather evenly distributed across all four levels of undergraduate school and 6 percent of the students in the study were in graduate school. Most students in the study lived either on campus (but not in a sorority or fraternity house) or off campus (but not with parents or relatives). The study contained more females than males. About two out of three students in the study were Caucasian (64%), while African Americans (11%) and Hispanics (13%) comprised significant percentages of students.

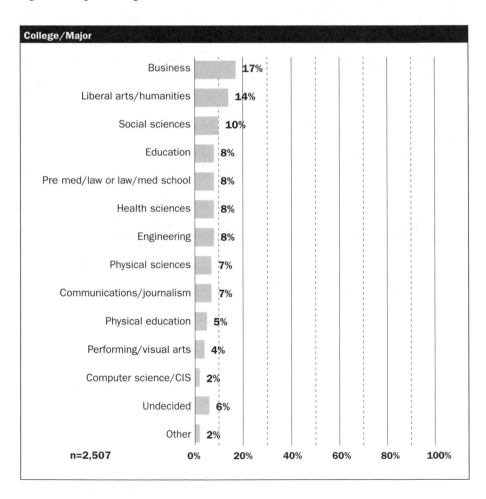

College/Major

Major	Percentage
Business	17%
Liberal arts/humanities	14%
Social sciences	10%
Education	8%
Pre med/law or law/med school	8%
Health sciences	8%
Engineering	8%
Physical sciences	7%
Communications/journalism	7%
Physical education	5%
Performing/visual arts	4%
Computer science/CIS	2%
Undecided	6%
Other	2%

n=2,507

Year in school

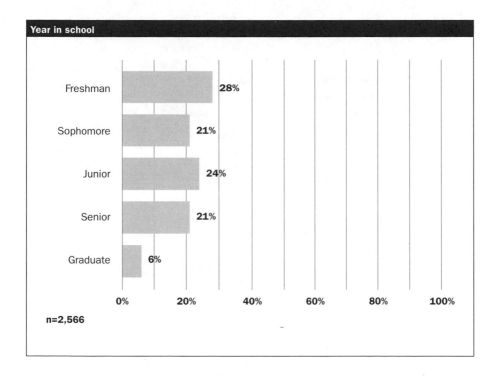

n=2,566

Housing

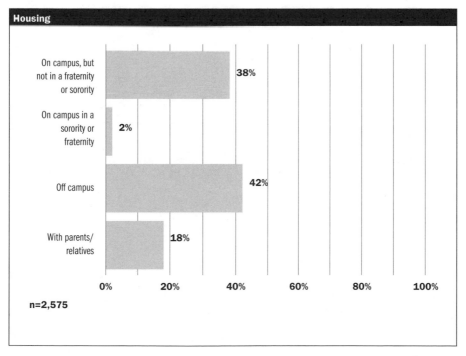

n=2,575

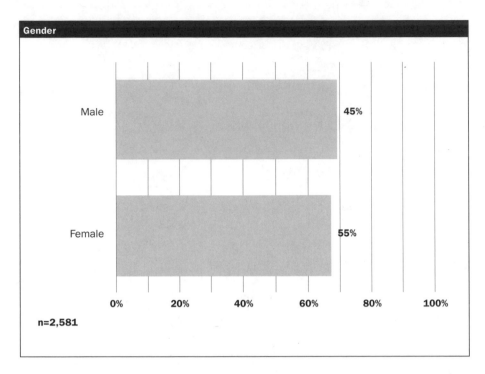

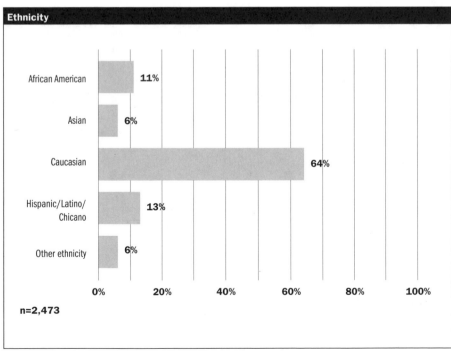

The Recreational Sports Expenditure Survey

Introduction

Purpose

This study was conducted for the National Intramural-Recreational Sports Association (NIRSA) by Kerr & Downs Research. The purpose of this study is to document the buying power and economic impact of NIRSA member colleges and universities. Specific attention was devoted to the following:

- Number of stand-alone and shared indoor and outdoor recreational centers/complexes
- Costs of new construction and renovation of indoor and outdoor recreational facilities
- Gross square footage of indoor recreational facilities,
- Number of outdoor playing fields
- Specific components (e.g. basketball courts, aquatics, etc.) of indoor and outdoor recreational facilities
- Number, estimated costs and estimated size of indoor and outdoor recreational facilities planned for the next five years
- Specific components of planned indoor and outdoor recreational facilities
- Dollars spent in the past fiscal year on specific, recurring expenditures such as game/sports equipment, apparel, field maintenance, etc.
- Dollars spent in the past ten years on periodic expenditures such as free weights, resurfacing, aquatics equipment, etc.
- Presence of food service operations, types of items sold and revenue generated
- Capital, operational and total budgets for recreational sports programs

Contributors to the Study

While Kerr & Downs Research accepts responsibility for limitations of the study related to methodology and implementation, many individuals made significant contributions to this research effort. NIRSA members Sid Gonsoulin, Director of Recreational Sports at University of Southern Mississippi and John Meyer, Associate Director of Recreational Sports at the University of Colorado, and Aaron Hill, Marketing Director for NIRSA, worked extensively with Kerr & Downs Research throughout the study. Without their direction and hands-on efforts, the study would not have been completed.

We also wish to thank the NIRSA board of directors who were in office during the planning and implementation of this research effort: Patti Bostic, President; Bill Sells, Past President; Brian Carswell, President-Elect; Patricia R. Besner, Past Presidents' Representative; Warren Isenhour, National Student Representative; Kent Blumenthal, Executive Director; Jeffrey S. Kearney, Region I Vice President; Sid Gonsoulin, Region II Vice President; Jan Wells, Region III Vice President; Warren Simpson, Region IV Vice President; Ron Seibring, Region V Vice President and Kathleen Hatch, Region VI Vice President, for their vision in advancing this study from concept to implementation.

Sincere appreciation is also extended to a Senior Advisory Group consisting of Judith Bryant, Jesse Clements, Mary Daniels, Michael Deluca, William Ehling, Mark Fletcher, Janet Gong, William Healey, Thomas Kirch, Gerald Maas, John Meyer, Eric Nickel, James Turman and Jeffrey Vessely. These individuals contributed their expertise toward sample composition and questionnaire issues.

Research Method

The study was conducted via mail, email and fax during April and May of 2002. A total of 681 NIRSA member colleges and 145 nonmember colleges received the questionnaire. A total of 198 total completed surveys were returned for a response rate of 24%. The sampling error given a 95% confidence level was ±6.1%. Results from this study have been extrapolated in many cases throughout this report to all NIRSA member colleges and universities.

Executive Summary

Profile of Existing Indoor & Outdoor Recreational Facilities

Existing Indoor Recreational Facilities. The typical college** had one stand-alone indoor recreational center/complex, yet 40% of colleges had none. The typical college also had one shared indoor recreational center/complex although 20% of colleges had none, and 35% had more than one.

> NIRSA member colleges have 560 stand-alone indoor complexes and 986 shared indoor complexes.*

Nearly half of the indoor stand-alone recreational complexes had been built or renovated since 1995; 25% since 2000. Average project cost for new construction for each indoor complex was $8.9 million, and it was $13.9 million for indoor complexes built since 2000. New construction cost per square foot since 2000 was $167.

Average project cost for indoor facility renovation was $4.4 million and it was $3.1 million for renovations completed since 2000. Renovation cost per square foot since 2000 was $111.

> New construction dollars spent by NIRSA member colleges on indoor recreational facilities totaled $7.331 billion. Total project costs for renovations were $2.291 billion. Total dollars spent on indoor recreational facilities in the past for new construction and renovation among NIRSA member colleges has been $9.6 billion.
>
> Since 2000, NIRSA member colleges have spent $5.367 billion on new construction of indoor recreational facilities and $1.192 billion on renovating indoor recreational facilities. Total dollars spent on indoor recreational facilities since 2000 for new construction and renovation among NIRSA member colleges has been $6.6 billion.

---

*Throughout this study, the results have been extrapolated to all NIRSA member colleges
** The term "college" will be used throughout to refer to colleges and universities.

The average number of square feet for indoor recreational complexes was 80,000. Indoor facility size was correlated to college size as facilities at small colleges had an average of 47,500 square feet; facilities at large colleges had, on average, 86,143 square feet.

NIRSA member colleges accounted for 91 million square feet of indoor recreational facilities.

Existing Outdoor Recreational Facilities. Three out of five NIRSA member colleges (62%) had at least one outdoor stand-alone field complex, and 68% of member colleges had at least one shared field complex.

NIRSA member colleges have 907 stand alone outdoor complexes and 1,052 shared outdoor complexes.

Over half (52%) of the outdoor recreational facilities have been built or renovated since 1995. Average new construction cost for all outdoor recreational facilities was $1.1 million, and for facilities built since 2000 it was $1.5 million. Average project costs for renovations of outdoor recreational facilities was $882,786. Seven out of ten (71%) outdoor recreational projects involved new construction; 29% involved renovations.

Total new construction dollars spent by NIRSA member colleges on outdoor recreational facilities has been $1.588 billion; $396.9 million since 2000. Total project costs for renovations has been $501.5 million; $125.4 million since 2000.

Total dollars spent on outdoor recreational facilities in the past for new construction and renovation among NIRSA member colleges has been $2.09 billion. Total dollars spent on outdoor recreational facilities since 2000 for new construction and renovation among NIRSA member colleges has been $522.3 million.

Nearly all colleges (97%) had outdoor fields and two out of three colleges (67%) had lighted outdoor fields. Across all NIRSA member colleges, there are 1,244 outdoor fields, 720 of which are lighted.

Total New Construction & Renovation Costs

Total dollars spent by NIRSA member colleges for new construction and renovation of all indoor and outdoor recreational complexes, centers and facilities has been $11.69 billion.

Total dollars spent by NIRSA member colleges for new construction and renovation of all indoor and outdoor recreational complexes, centers and facilities since 2000 has been $7.12 billion.

Components of Existing Indoor & Outdoor Facilities

Indoor Recreational Centers/Complexes. Percentages of colleges with various components within their indoor recreational facilities are shown below.

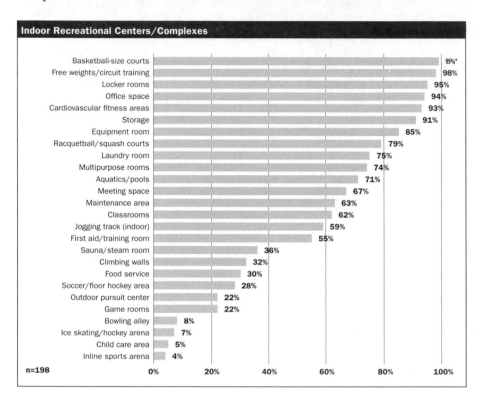

Indoor Recreational Centers/Complexes

Component	Percentage
Basketball-size courts	99%*
Free weights/circuit training	98%
Locker rooms	95%
Office space	94%
Cardiovascular fitness areas	93%
Storage	91%
Equipment room	85%
Racquetball/squash courts	79%
Laundry room	75%
Multipurpose rooms	74%
Aquatics/pools	71%
Meeting space	67%
Maintenance area	63%
Classrooms	62%
Jogging track (indoor)	59%
First aid/training room	55%
Sauna/steam room	36%
Climbing walls	32%
Food service	30%
Soccer/floor hockey area	28%
Outdoor pursuit center	22%
Game rooms	22%
Bowling alley	8%
Ice skating/hockey arena	7%
Child care area	5%
Inline sports arena	4%

n=198

The total number of component units for indoor recreational sports facilities for all NIRSA member colleges were:

- 3,881 basketball courts
- 3,816 racquetball/squash courts
- 1,088 multipurpose rooms
- 246 climbing walls
- 476 bowling lanes
- 696 aquatics/pools
- 185 game rooms

Outdoor Recreational Facilities. Percentages of colleges with various components within their outdoor recreational facilities are shown below.

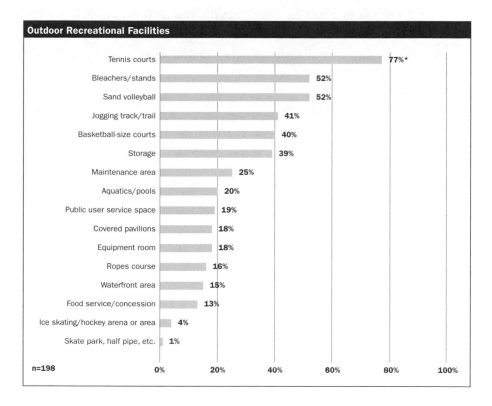

Outdoor Recreational Facilities

Component	Percentage
Tennis courts	77%*
Bleachers/stands	52%
Sand volleyball	52%
Jogging track/trail	41%
Basketball-size courts	40%
Storage	39%
Maintenance area	25%
Aquatics/pools	20%
Public user service space	19%
Covered pavilions	18%
Equipment room	18%
Ropes course	16%
Waterfront area	15%
Food service/concession	13%
Ice skating/hockey arena or area	4%
Skate park, half pipe, etc.	1%

n=198

Total number of component units for outdoor recreational sports facilities for all NIRSA member colleges were:

- 868 basketball courts
- 4,851 tennis courts
- 1,890 covered pavilions
- 210 aquatics/pools

Nearly all colleges (97%) had flag football-size outdoor fields; 71% of colleges had lighted outdoor fields.

Profile of Planned Indoor & Outdoor Recreational Facilities

Planned Indoor Recreational Facilities. NIRSA member college plan to build or renovate 400 indoor recreational facilities over the next five years. Three out of five (60%) will involve new construction.

The average **new construction** cost for an indoor **recreational** facility over the next five years will be $12.7 million. The average cost for the renovation of an indoor recreational facility over the next five years will be $8.4 million.

Total new construction costs for indoor recreational facilities for NIRSA member colleges over the next five years will be $3.037 billion; total renovation costs over the same time period for indoor recreational facilities will be $1.344 billion.

> **Total new construction and renovation costs for indoor recreational facilities for NIRSA member colleges over the next five years will be $4.381 billion.**

> **NIRSA member colleges plan 28.8 million square feet of new construction and renovations for their indoor recreational facilities over the next five years.**

Planned Outdoor Recreational Facilities. NIRSA member colleges will build or renovate 318 outdoor recreational facilities over the next five years. Seven out of ten (69%) will involve new construction. There are 721 flag football-size fields planned among NIRSA member colleges over the next five years. Five hundred eighty (580) of the planned fields will be lighted.

> **There are 721 flag football-size fields planned among NIRSA member colleges over the next five years.**

The average new construction cost for an outdoor recreational facility over the next five years will be $1.55 million. The average cost for the renovation of an outdoor recreational facility over the next five years will be $2.14 million.

Total new construction costs for outdoor recreational facilities for NIRSA colleges over the next five years will be $340.83 million; total renovation costs over the same time period for outdoor recreational facilities will be $210.58 million.

> **Total new construction and renovation costs for outdoor recreational facilities for NIRSA member colleges over the next five years will be $551.41 million.**

Components of Planned Indoor & Outdoor Facilities

Indoor Recreational Centers/Complexes. Percentages of colleges with various components within their indoor recreational facilities that are planned for the next five years are shown below.

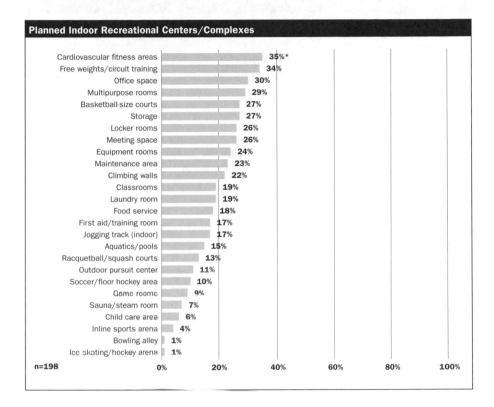

Total numbers of new and renovated component units planned for indoor recreational sports facilities for all NIRSA member colleges over the next five years were:

- 794 basketball courts
- 533 racquetball/squash courts
- 574 multipurpose rooms
- 182 climbing walls
- 170 aquatics/pools
- 70 game rooms

Outdoor Recreational Facilities. Percentages of colleges with various components within their outdoor recreational facilities that are planned for the next five years are shown below.

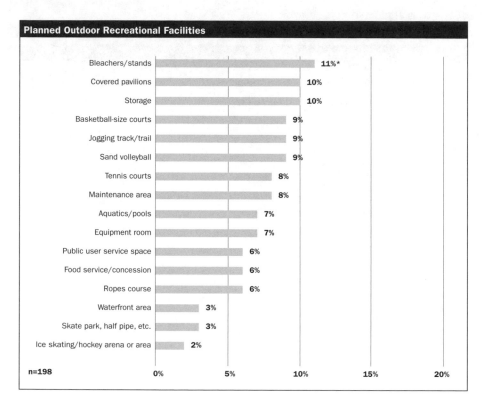

Planned Outdoor Recreational Facilities

Facility	Percentage
Bleachers/stands	11%*
Covered pavilions	10%
Storage	10%
Basketball-size courts	9%
Jogging track/trail	9%
Sand volleyball	9%
Tennis courts	8%
Maintenance area	8%
Aquatics/pools	7%
Equipment room	7%
Public user service space	6%
Food service/concession	6%
Ropes course	6%
Waterfront area	3%
Skate park, half pipe, etc.	3%
Ice skating/hockey arena or area	2%

n=198

Total numbers of new and renovated component units planned for outdoor recreational sports facilities for all NIRSA member colleges over the next five years were:

144 basketball courts
408 tennis courts
74 covered pavilions
55 aquatics/pools

Nearly all of the NIRSA colleges (98%) that reported data planned to add outdoor flag football-sized fields; nearly nine out of ten colleges (88%) planned to add lighted outdoor flag football-sized fields in the next five years.

Annual Expenditures

Total expenditures for all NIRSA member colleges during the most recent fiscal year are shown in the table below.

Expenditures During Most Recent Fiscal Year						
			PERCENTILES			
EXPENSE CATEGORIES	10th	25th	50th	75th	90TH	MEAN
Recreational sporting equipment						
Games/sports equipment	$500	$1,200	$3,000	$10,000	$25,000	$10,715
Goals, nets, mats, pads, etc.	$200	$556	$2,000	$5,000	$10,000	$3,928
Apparel	$400	$1,500	$3,000	$6,000	$14,700	$5,699
Outdoor recreation equipment	$0	$500	$2,000	$5,000	$20,00	$7,467
Other recreational sporting equip.	$700	$2,500	$5,000	$30,000	$66,532	$19,445
Facilities operations						
Video/audio/entertainment systems, cardio theater, etc.	$0	$350	$2,000	$5,000	$10,000	$7,028
First Aid, medical supplies	$100	$288	$800	$2,000	$5,000	$1,887
Utilities	$0	$9,000	$114,600	$300,000	$552,000	$203,102
General maintenance and janitorial supplies	$440	$3,000	$20,000	$55,486	$125,000	$57,112
Floor maintenance, resealing surfaces, carpeting, etc.	$800	$2,800	$10,000	$19,533	$39,000	$15,160
Field maintenance, fences, back-stops, goals, landscaping, etc.	$18	$1,000	$4,500	$18,125	$50,000	$18,604
Safety and security	$0	$1,000	$2,500	$10,000	$20,000	$8,062
Facility components	$0	$500	$2,000	$5,750	$24,500	$11,281
Other facilities operations	$1,180	$3,185	$9,488	$76,750	$194,000	$82,301
Administration						
Computers/software/technical	$360	$1,500	$5,000	$12,000	$26,560	$25,296
Marketing/promotions/incentives	$275	$1,000	$3,000	$9,000	$24,255	$11,830
Office supplies/equipment	$300	$800	$2,500	$10,000	$29,800	$10,376
Consultants/contractual services	$0	$325	$5,500	$15,000	$47,470	$17,044
Salaries and wages	$18,400	$68,000	$200,000	$700,000	$1,200,000	$482,610
Dues, memberships, publications	$300	$500	$1,000	$2,000	$4,000	$2,134
Other administration	$1,400	$4,450	$17,000	$85,000	$560,000	$116,078
Miscellaneous						
Appliances/furniture	$0	$350	$2,000	$6,000	$25,000	$11,959
Child care facilities/services	$0	$0	$0	$0	$0	$0
Travel	$500	$1,725	$5,000	$11,461	$32,610	$12,554
Other miscellaneous	$1,015	$4,504	$10,000	$22,750	$1,745,910	$287,722

Infrequent Expenditures

Total expenditures for all NIRSA member colleges for items, products, services, etc. that are not purchased every year are shown in the table below.

Total Expenditures — Past 10 Years	
Free weights/weight training circuit equipment	$93,212,000
Video/audio/entertainment systems, cardio theater, electronics	$12,261,200
Cardiovascular equipment	$89,786,200
Laundry and maintenance	$19,876,500
Miscellaneous facility equipment (standards, goal, netting, padding, backboards, curtains, etc.	$31,487,400
Resurfacing (courts, lanes, rooms, etc.)	$61,107,800
Architectural services	$94,275,720
Aquatics equipment	$24,761,800
Lighting	$108,398,500
Other infrequently purchased items	$12,867,400

Total **planned** purchases over the next five years for all NIRSA member colleges for items, products, services, etc. that are not purchased every year are shown in the table below.

Total Expenditures — Next 5 years	
Free weights/weight training circuit equipment	$58,855,300
Video/audio/entertainment systems, cardio theater, electronics	$12,741,400
Cardiovascular equipment	$81,855,900
Laundry and maintenance	$13,427,400
Miscellaneous facility equipment (standards, goal, netting, padding, backboards, curtains, etc.	$17,325,000
Resurfacing (courts, lanes, rooms, etc.)	$41,867,000
Architectural services	$66,348,000
Aquatics equipment	$20,711,600
Lighting	$99,675,100
Other infrequently purchased items	$22,445,486

Food Service

Nearly half of NIRSA member colleges (46%) have food service operations as part of the recreational sports area. Most colleges that have food service outsource either all (78%) or part (13%) of their food service operation. Soft drinks (32%), bottled water (32%) and chips, pretzels and other snacks (28%) were the items carried by the highest percentage of NIRSA members. Soft drinks, bottled water and fruit drinks, smoothies, health drinks, etc. were the food service items with the highest unit sales.

Recreational Sports Budgets

Average operational, capital and total budgets for NIRSA member colleges were:

Average Operational Budget $862,000
Average Capital Budget $540,000
Average Total Budget $1,368,000

The sum of all NIRSA member colleges' budgets were:
Operational Budgets: .... $603.4 million
Capital Budgets: .... $378.0 million
Total Budgets: .... $957.6 million

Information on Colleges and Universities in the Study

The typical college in the study had 5,900 full-time and 2,400 part-time students. More than one-in-seven colleges (15%) had more than 20,000 students. The typical Director of Campus Recreation who responded to the study had six years in his/her current position, 11 years at his/her current college, and 17 years in recreational sports.

> Nine-out-of-ten colleges (91%) had a Director of Recreational Sports job position, while half of the colleges had an Assistant Director and 40% had an Associate Director. Four-in-ten-colleges had a Coordinator.

Nearly all Directors had purchasing authority with the typical Director authorized to purchase $5,000 worth of products or services. Four out of five Assistant Directors (78%) and Associate Directors (81%) had purchasing authority, and they were authorized to purchase $2,000 and $5,000 worth of products and services, respectively. Just over three out of five Coordinators (63%) had purchasing authority with $2,500 being the limit for the typical Coordinator.

> Nearly half of colleges in the study (45%) permitted paid outdoor promotional signs or boards. Three out of five colleges (62%) permitted paid indoor promotional signs or boards.

Findings

Background and Profile Information

Experience of Recreation Directors

Current Position. The typical Campus Recreation Director had six years of experience in his/her current position. One-in-four Campus Recreation Directors (26%) had been in his/her current position two or fewer years, while nearly one-in-five (18%) had more than 15 years of experience. One in eight Campus Recreation Directors (12%) responding to this study had only one year of experience in his/her current position.

At Current College. The typical Campus Recreation Director had been at his/her college for 11 years. Nearly one-in-five Campus Recreation Directors (19%) had been at his/her college for two or fewer years, while one-in-five (21%) had been at his/her college for more than 20 years. Slightly fewer than one-in-ten (9%) of Campus Recreation Directors had been at their current colleges only one year.

In Recreational Sports. The typical Campus Recreation Director had worked in recreational sports for 17 years. Fifteen percent (15%) of Campus Recreation Directors had been in the business for five or fewer years, while two out of five Campus Recreation Directors (39%) had been in the recreational sports arena for more than 20 years.

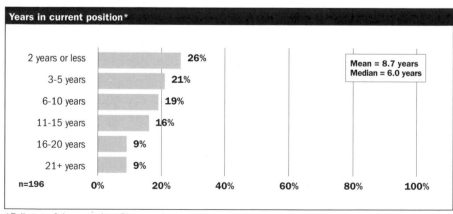

*Full text of the question: Please write in how many years you have worked at your current position.

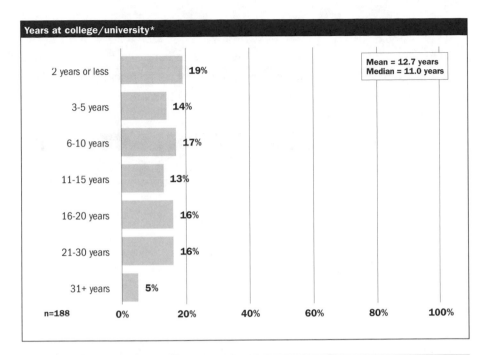

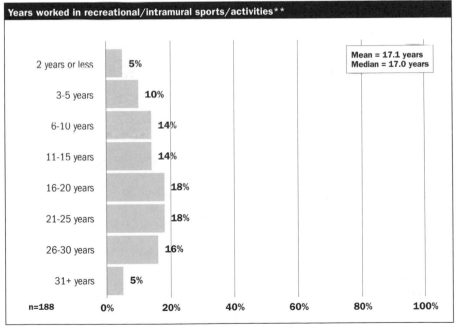

*Full text of the question: Please write in how many years you have worked at your college/university.
** Full text of the question: Please write in how many years you have worked in recreational/intamural sports/activities.

College Enrollment

The typical college represented in this study had approximately 5,900 full-time and 2,400 part-time students. However, 15% of the colleges had over 20,000 full-time students. Over half of the colleges (52%) had fewer than 2,500 part-time students.

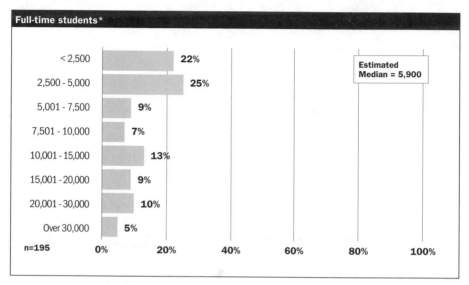

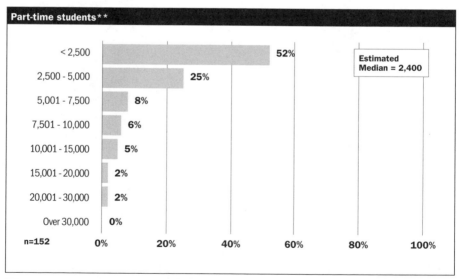

*Full text of the question: Check the responses that reflect how many full-time students attend your college/unversity.

**Full text of the question: Check the responses that reflect how many part-time students attend your college/university.

Region

All NIRSA regions were represented in the study with slightly more colleges from Region 4 (21%) and Region 2 (20%).

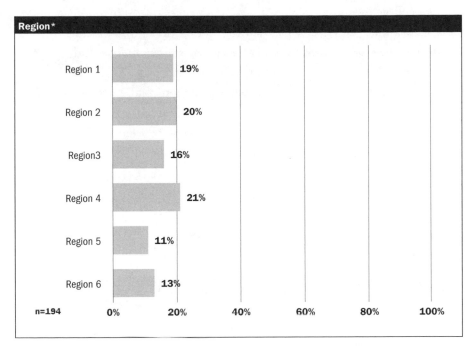

*Full text of the question: In which state is your college located?

NIRSA regions include the following states by region:

Region 1: Connecticut, Delaware, District of Columbia, Maine, Maryland, Massachusetts, New Hampshire, New Jersey, New York, Pennsylvania, Rhode Island, and Vermont

Region 2: Alabama, Florida, Georgia, Kentucky, Mississippi, North Carolina, South Carolina, Tennessee, Virginia, and West Virginia

Region 3: Illinois, Indiana, Michigan, Ohio, and Wisconsin

Region 4: Arakansas, Kansas, Louisiana, Missouri, New Mexico, Oklahoma, and Texas

Region 5: Colorado, Iowa, Minnesota, Montana, Nebraska, North Dakota, South Dakota and Wyoming

Region 6: Alaska, Arizona, California, Hawaii, Idaho, Nevada, Oregon, Utah, and Washington

Existing Campus Recreation Centers/Complexes

Campus Recreation Directors were asked to indicate the number of indoor and outdoor stand-alone and shared recreational centers/complexes there were on their college campuses. Three out of five colleges (60%) had *indoor, stand-alone* recreational centers/complexes with most of these (47%) having just one. Four out of five colleges (80%) had at least one *shared, indoor* student recreational center/complex with a plurality (45%) of campuses having just one.

Over three out of five colleges (62%) had one or more outdoor, stand-alone field complexes and 27% of colleges had at least two. Two out of three campuses (68%) had one or more *shared, outdoor* field complexes, while 36% had more than one.

Projecting numbers from the study to all NIRSA member colleges results in the numbers of centers/complexes and field complexes (mean in parentheses) shown below.

TOTAL INDOOR		TOTAL OUTDOOR	
Stand-alone centers/complexes	Shared complexes	Stand-alone centers/complexes	Shared complexes
560 (.8)	986 (1.41)	907 (1.3)	1,052 (1.51)

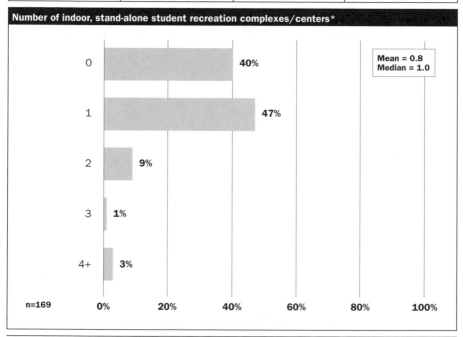

Number of indoor, stand-alone student recreation complexes/centers*

Mean = 0.8
Median = 1.0

- 0 — 40%
- 1 — 47%
- 2 — 9%
- 3 — 1%
- 4+ — 3%

n=169

*Full text of the question: Please write in the number of indoor and outdoor stand-alone and shared (with another discipline, department) recreational centers/complexes your college has. (Write 0 if your college has none.)

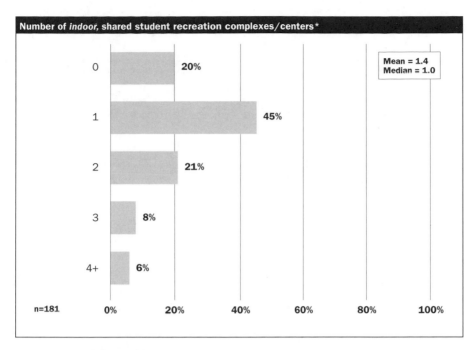

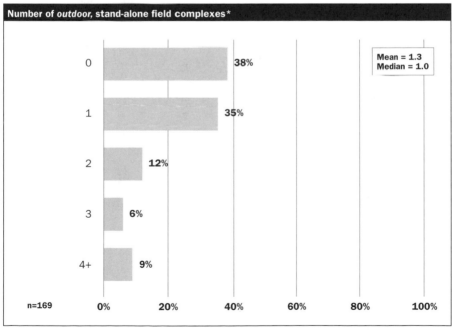

*Full text of the question: Please write in the number of indoor and outdoor stand-alone and shared (with another discipline, department) recreational centers/complexes your college has. (Write 0 if your college has none.)

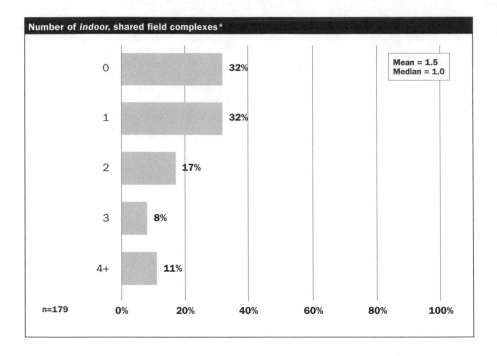

Number of *indoor*, shared field complexes*

0	32%
1	32%
2	17%
3	8%
4+	11%

Mean = 1.5
Median = 1.0

n=179

0%   20%   40%   60%   80%   100%

*Full text of the question: Please write in the number of indoor and outdoor stand-alone and shared (with another discipline, department) recreational centers/complexes your college has. (Write 0 if your college has none.)

Specifications of Indoor Facilities

This section deals with the year each indoor facility was completed or renovated, its cost, whether it was a renovation or new construction, a brief description of the facility and its gross square footage.

Year Built. The 198 colleges in the study reported statistics on 322 indoor campus recreational facilities. The oldest was built in 1905. One-in-four indoor campus recreation facilities (25%) had been built or renovated since 2000. The same exact percentage (25%) of indoor facilities had been built or renovated prior to 1980; 5% of the indoor recreational facilities were built or renovated prior to 1950. Yet there had been a flurry of building and renovation since 1995 with nearly half of the indoor facilities (45%) having been built or renovated since that date.

Project Cost. Building and renovation project costs for the indoor recreational facilities reported in this study ranged from $8,000 to $100,000,000 with the typical (50th percentile) project cost being $4,500,000. Given the presence of several high-end projects, the average project cost was considerably larger than the typical project cost. The average project cost was $7,185,000. Translating the project costs in this study to all NIRSA member colleges results in total project costs for indoor recreational facilities of $9.6 billion.

The project cost for the typical renovation was $1,000,000 while the project cost for typical new construction was $6,000,000. Average costs for renovations and new construction were $4,359,192 and $8,857,721, respectively. New construction completed since 2000 had average and median project costs of $13,885,395 and $10,500,000 respectively.

Median project costs for small, large and all colleges are shown below.

$4,500,000 All colleges
$5,150,000 Large colleges
$3,500,000 Small colleges

Renovation vs. New Construction. Two out of three facilities (66%) reported in this study were new construction. Large colleges were more likely than small ones (75% to 60%) to report new construction, while small colleges had comparatively more renovations. Cost per square foot of new construction built since 2000 was $167, while cost per square foot for renovations completed since 2000 was $111.

Description of Building/Renovation Projects. Over half of the indoor facilities referenced by participants in the study were athletic buildings or recreational centers (56%). About one in seven indoor facilities (15%) were gymnasiums, while pools/aquatic centers and gymnasium-oriented equipment were both mentioned 14% of the time.

Gross Square Footage. Gross square footage of indoor recreational facilities reported in this study ranged from 700 to 400,000. The typical (50th percentile) indoor recreational facility had 62,000 square feet and the average facility had 80,000 square feet. Median square footage for indoor recreational facilities for small, large and all colleges in the study are shown below:

    62,000 All colleges
    47,500 Small colleges
    86,143 Large colleges

Applying the results of this study to all NIRSA member colleges translates into 91 million square feet of indoor recreational facilities.

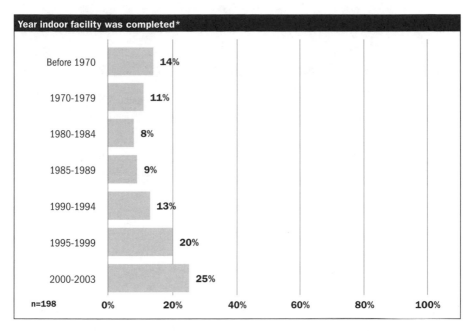

Year indoor facility was completed*

Before 1970	14%
1970-1979	11%
1980-1984	8%
1985-1989	9%
1990-1994	13%
1995-1999	20%
2000-2003	25%

n=198

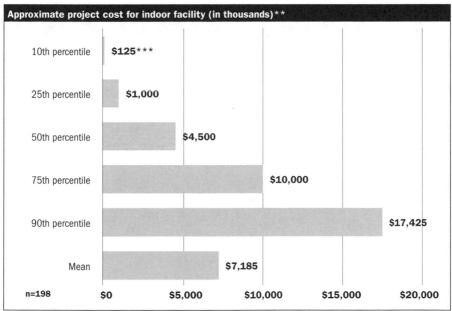

Approximate project cost for indoor facility (in thousands)**

10th percentile	$125***
25th percentile	$1,000
50th percentile	$4,500
75th percentile	$10,000
90th percentile	$17,425
Mean	$7,185

n=198

*Full text of the question: Please write the year the facilities your campus uses for campus recreation were last built or renovated. (Do NOT include future projects.)

**Full text of the question: Write down the approximate cost of the construction or renovation. You may use a range (e.g., $3 to $3.5 million) if you do not have specific numbers.

***10% of the indoor recreational facilities cost less than $125,000 to build or renovate.

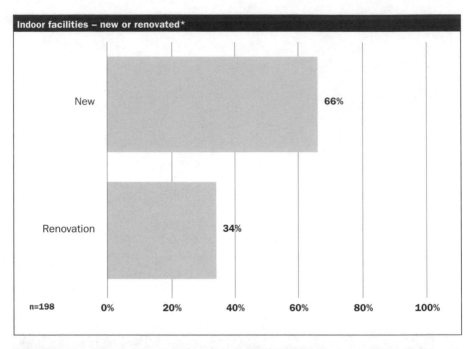

Indoor facilities – new or renovated*

New 66%

Renovation 34%

n=198

0%   20%   40%   60%   80%   100%

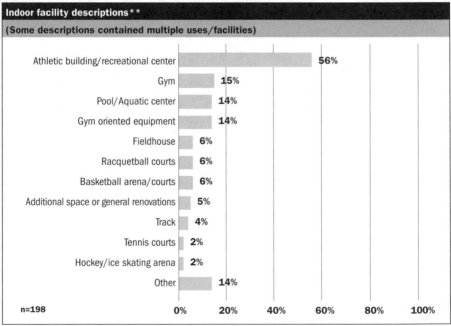

Indoor facility descriptions*

(Some descriptions contained multiple uses/facilities)

Athletic building/recreational center 56%
Gym 15%
Pool/Aquatic center 14%
Gym oriented equipment 14%
Fieldhouse 6%
Racquetball courts 6%
Basketball arena/courts 6%
Additional space or general renovations 5%
Track 4%
Tennis courts 2%
Hockey/ice skating arena 2%
Other 14%

n=198

0%   20%   40%   60%   80%   100%

* Full text of the question: Write an "N" or "R" if you are referencing New construction or Renovation.
** A complete list of the descriptions can be found in the Appendix.

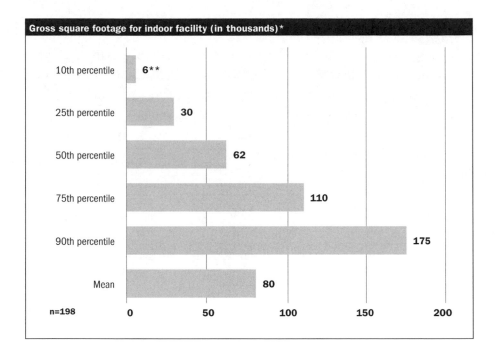

Gross square footage for indoor facility (in thousands)*

10th percentile	6**
25th percentile	30
50th percentile	62
75th percentile	110
90th percentile	175
Mean	80

n=198

0   50   100   150   200

* Full text of the question: Write in the gross square footage for each indoor facility.
** 10% of indoor recreational facilities had 6,000 or fewer square feet.

Components of Indoor Facilities

Graphs on pages 122 and 123 show the percentages of colleges that have specific components within their indoor recreational centers/complexes. Nearly all colleges (99%) have basketball size courts within their indoor facilities, and 98% have free weights/circuit weight training areas. At least nine out of ten colleges have within their indoor recreational centers/complexes other facilities which include locker rooms (95%), office space (94%), cardiovascular fitness areas (93%) and storage (91%).

At least seven out of ten colleges have equipment rooms (85%), racquetball/squash courts (79%), laundry rooms (75%), multipurpose rooms (74%), and aquatics/pools (71%) within their indoor recreational centers/complexes. Comparatively few colleges have the following within their indoor recreational centers/complexes:

4% Inline sports arena
5% Child care area
7% Ice skating/hockey arena or area
8% Bowling alley

Components of Indoor Facilities by Size of College

The table on the following page compares the percentages of small and large colleges that have various components within their indoor recreational facilities.

As expected, indoor recreational facilities in larger colleges were more likely to have these components than facilities at smaller colleges. There were exceptions including First Aid/training rooms, game rooms, inline sports arenas and food service.

For certain components such as basketball courts, Campus Recreational Directors were requested to indicate the number that were contained within their indoor recreational centers/complexes. The following are the average numbers:

4.6 Basketball courts
6.9 Racquetball/squash courts
2.1 Multipurpose rooms
1.1 Climbing walls
8.5 Bowling lanes
1.4 Aquatics/pools
1.2 Game rooms

Across all NIRSA member colleges/universities, these numbers translate into the following total number of units:

3,881 Basketball courts

3,816 Racquetball/squash courts

1,088 Multipurpose rooms

246 Climbing walls

476 Bowling lanes

696 Aquatics/pools

185 Game rooms

INDOOR RECREATIONAL COMPONENTS	ALL COLLEGES	SMALL COLLEGES	LARGE COLLEGES
Basketball-size courts	99%	98%	100%
Free weights/circuit training	98%	93%	100%
Locker rooms	95%	88%	97%
Office space	94%	88%	100%
Cardiovascular fitness areas	93%	88%	100%
Storage	91%	91%	100%
Equipment room	85%	83%	93%
Racquetball/squash courts	79%	69%	97%
Laundry room	75%	69%	79%
Multipurpose rooms	74%	62%	90%
Aquatics/pools	71%	45%	86%
Meeting space	67%	55%	79%
Maintenance area	63%	62%	86%
Classrooms	62%	52%	76%
Jogging track (indoor)	59%	50%	79%
First Aid/training room	55%	64%	55%
Sauna/steam room	36%	26%	52%
Climbing walls	32%	21%	59%
Food service	30%	38%	31%
Soccer/floor hockey area	28%	29%	41%
Outdoor pursuit center	22%	7%	52%
Game rooms	22%	29%	21%
Bolwing alley	8%	7%	10%
Ice skating/hockey arena or area	7%	2%	17%
Child care area	5%	5%	7%
Inline sports arena	4%	5%	3%

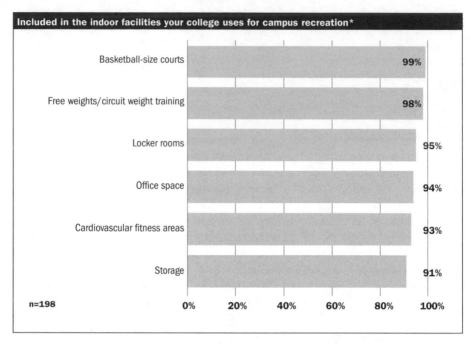

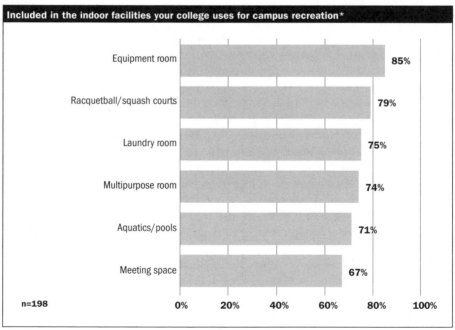

*Full text of the question: What is included in the indoor facilities your college uses for campus recreation?

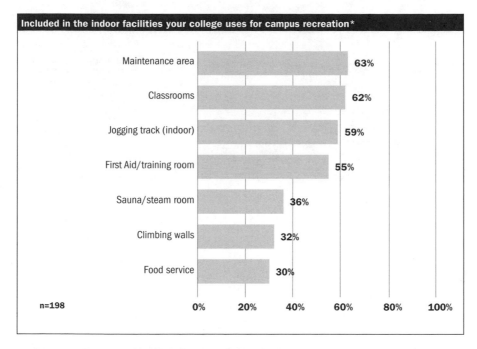

Included in the indoor facilities your college uses for campus recreation*

- Maintenance area — 63%
- Classrooms — 62%
- Jogging track (indoor) — 59%
- First Aid/training room — 55%
- Sauna/steam room — 36%
- Climbing walls — 32%
- Food service — 30%

n=198

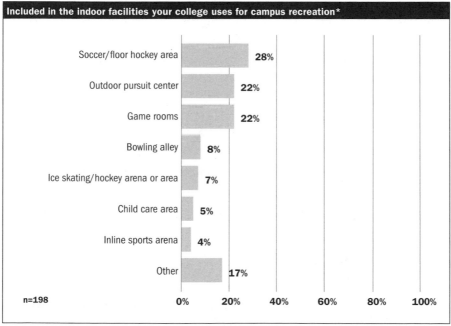

Included in the indoor facilities your college uses for campus recreation*

- Soccer/floor hockey area — 28%
- Outdoor pursuit center — 22%
- Game rooms — 22%
- Bowling alley — 8%
- Ice skating/hockey arena or area — 7%
- Child care area — 5%
- Inline sports arena — 4%
- Other — 17%

n=198

*Full text of the question: What is included in the indoor facilities your college uses for campus recreation?

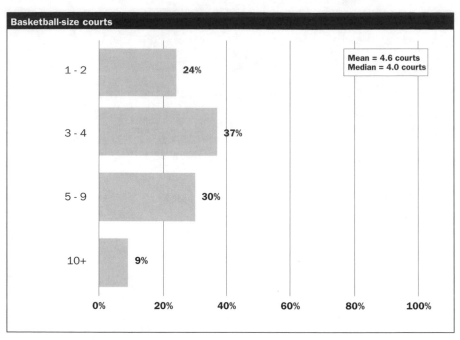

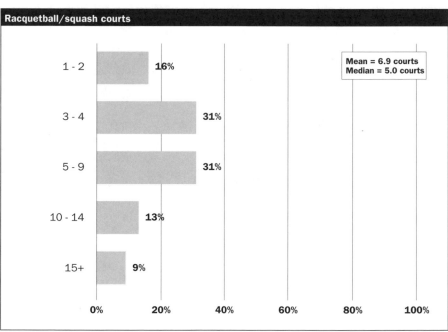

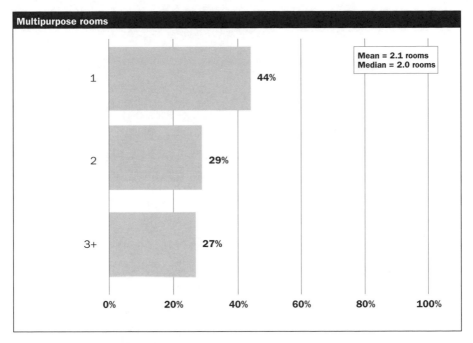

Multipurpose rooms

Mean = 2.1 rooms
Median = 2.0 rooms

1 — 44%

2 — 29%

3+ — 27%

0% 20% 40% 60% 80% 100%

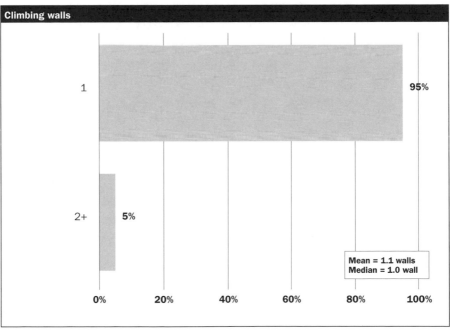

Climbing walls

1 — 95%

2+ — 5%

Mean = 1.1 walls
Median = 1.0 wall

0% 20% 40% 60% 80% 100%

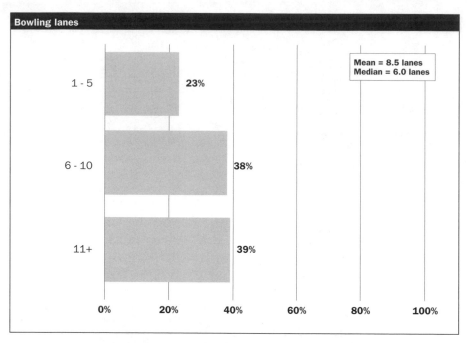

Bowling lanes

1 - 5   23%

6 - 10   38%

11+   39%

Mean = 8.5 lanes
Median = 6.0 lanes

0%   20%   40%   60%   80%   100%

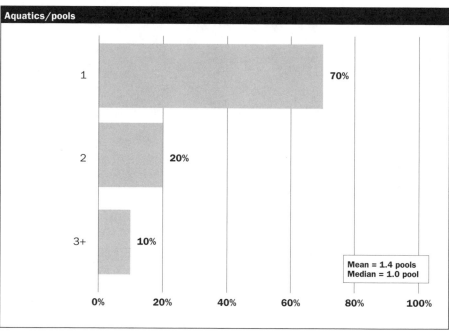

Aquatics/pools

1   70%

2   20%

3+   10%

Mean = 1.4 pools
Median = 1.0 pool

0%   20%   40%   60%   80%   100%

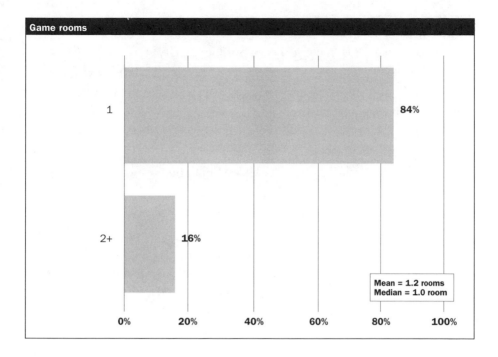

Specifications of Outdoor Facilities

This section deals with the year each outdoor facility was completed or renovated, its cost, whether it was a renovation or new construction, a brief description of the facility and the number of lighted fields and the number of total outdoor fields (flag football-size fields).

Year Built. The 198 colleges in the study reported statistics on 236 outdoor campus recreational facilities. The oldest was built in 1910. One-in-four outdoor campus recreation facilities (25%) had been built or renovated since 2000. One-in-six outdoor facilities (17%) had been built or renovated prior to 1980; 4% of the outdoor recreational facilities were built or renovated prior to 1960. Yet there had been significant building and renovation since 1995, with over half of the outdoor facilities (52%) having been built or renovated since that date.

Project Cost. Building and renovation project costs for the outdoor recreational facilities reported in this study ranged from $270 to $20,000,000 with the typical (50th percentile) project cost being $400,000. Given the presence of several high-end projects, the average project cost was considerably higher than the typical project cost. The average project cost was $1,055,000. Extrapolating the project costs in this study to all NIRSA member colleges resulted in total project costs of $880 million for outdoor recreational facilities.

The project cost for the typical **renovation** was $300,000, while the project cost for typical **new construction** was $400,000. Average costs for renovations and new construction were $882,786 and $1,141,358, respectively. New construction completed since 2000 had average and median project costs of $1,502,706 and $400,000, respectively.

Median project costs for small, large and all colleges are shown below.

   $400,000   All colleges
$1,000,000   Large colleges
    $75,000   Small colleges

Renovation vs. New Construction. Seven out of ten outdoor recreational facilities (71%) reported in this study were new construction. Smaller colleges were slightly more likely than larger ones (71% to 67%) to report new construction, while larger colleges had slightly more renovations. Cost per lighted field of new construction built since 2000 was $150,000, while cost per lighted field for renovations completed since 2000 was $70,000. Cost per field of new construction

built since 2000 was $106,250, while cost per lighted field for renovations com-
pleted since 2000 was $42,500.

Description of Building/Renovation Projects. The most frequently mentioned
outdoor recreational facility in the study was a multipurpose field (39%). Three-
in-ten colleges (30%) listed fields for specific sports and one-in-ten (10%) listed
tennis courts.

Number of Fields. Nearly all colleges (97%) had outdoor fields and two out
of three colleges (67%) had lighted outdoor fields. Each college had, on average,
3.6 lighted and 6.3 total outdoor (flag football size) fields. Extrapolating from the
figures in this study, NIRSA member colleges have 1,244 outdoor fields, 720 of
which are lighted.

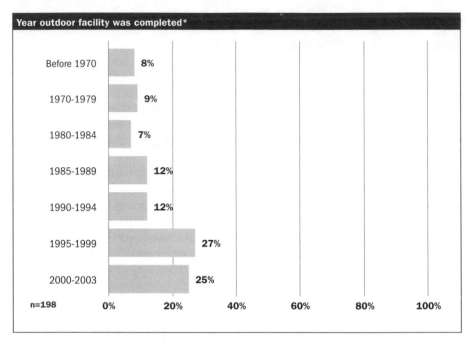

Year outdoor facility was completed*

Before 1970	8%
1970-1979	9%
1980-1984	7%
1985-1989	12%
1990-1994	12%
1995-1999	27%
2000-2003	25%

n=198

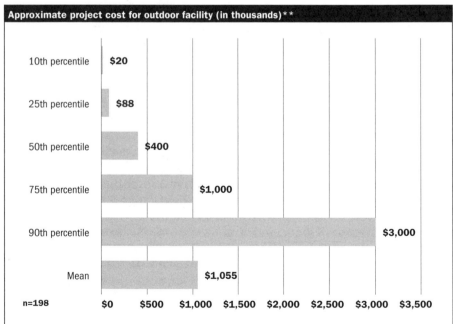

Approximate project cost for outdoor facility (in thousands)**

10th percentile	$20
25th percentile	$88
50th percentile	$400
75th percentile	$1,000
90th percentile	$3,000
Mean	$1,055

n=198

*Full text of the question: Please write the year the facilities your campus uses for campus recreation were last built or renovated. (Do NOT include future projects).
**Full text of the question: Write down the approximate cost of the construction or renovation. You may use a range (e.g., $3 to $3.5 million) if you do not have specific numbers.

Outdoor facilities – new or renovation*

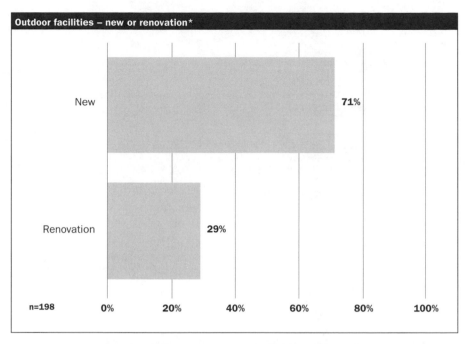

New 71%

Renovation 29%

n=198 0% 20% 40% 60% 80% 100%

Outdoor facility descriptions**
(Some descriptions contained multiple uses/facilities)

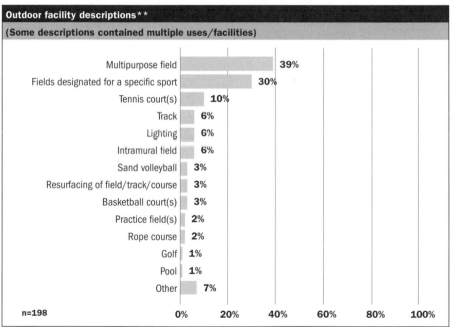

Multipurpose field 39%
Fields designated for a specific sport 30%
Tennis court(s) 10%
Track 6%
Lighting 6%
Intramural field 6%
Sand volleyball 3%
Resurfacing of field/track/course 3%
Basketball court(s) 3%
Practice field(s) 2%
Rope course 2%
Golf 1%
Pool 1%
Other 7%

n=198 0% 20% 40% 60% 80% 100%

*Full text of the question: Write an "N" or "R" if you are referencing New construction or Renovation.
**A complete list of the descriptions can be found in the Appendix.

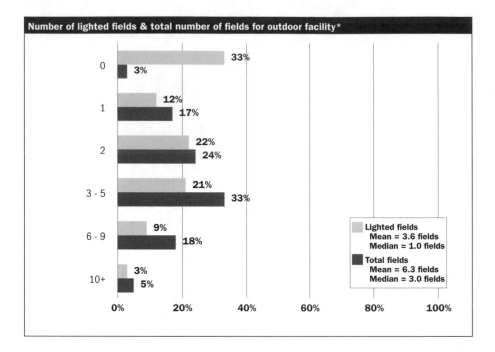

Number of lighted fields & total number of fields for outdoor facility*

- 0: Lighted fields 33%, Total fields 3%
- 1: Lighted fields 12%, Total fields 17%
- 2: Lighted fields 22%, Total fields 24%
- 3 - 5: Lighted fields 21%, Total fields 33%
- 6 - 9: Lighted fields 9%, Total fields 18%
- 10+: Lighted fields 3%, Total fields 5%

Lighted fields
Mean = 3.6 fields
Median = 1.0 fields

Total fields
Mean = 6.3 fields
Median = 3.0 fields

*Full text of the question: Write down the number of lighted and total number of a flag football-sized fields for each outdoor facility.

Components of Outdoor Facilities

Graphs on page 135 show what percentages of colleges have various components in their outdoor recreational facilities. Three out of four colleges (77%) had tennis courts with the average number of courts per college being 9.5. Just over half of the colleges had sand volleyball (52%) and bleachers/stands (52%). Two out of five colleges (41%) had jogging tracks or trails and nearly as many had basketball size courts (40%), and outdoor storage facilities (39%). One-in-four colleges had an outdoor maintenance area, and the other outdoor components appeared on no more than one-in-five campuses.

Outdoor recreational components	All Colleges	Small Colleges	Large Colleges
Tennis courts	77%	81%	97%
Bleachers/stands	52%	57%	69%
Sand volleyball	52%	52%	69%
Jogging track/trail	41%	38%	59%
Basketball-size courts	40%	31%	62%
Storage	39%	33%	59%
Maintenance area	25%	19%	55%
Aquatics/pools	20%	17%	45%
Public user service space	19%	14%	28%
Covered pavilions	18%	17%	24%
Equipment room	18%	17%	31%
Ropes course	16%	5%	35%
Waterfront area	15%	17%	28%
Food service/concession	13%	19%	14%
Ice skating/hockey arena or area	4%	2%	14%
Skate park, half pipe, etc.	1%	0%	0%

As expected, outdoor recreational facilities in larger colleges were more likely to have components than facilities at smaller colleges, as shown in the table on page 133. Smaller colleges were more likely to have food service concessions with their outdoor recreational facilities, and neither small nor large colleges had any skate parks (two midsized colleges had skate parks).

For certain components such as basketball courts, Campus Recreational Directors were requested to indicate the number that were contained in their outdoor recreational centers/complexes. The following are the average numbers:

3.1 Basketball courts
9.5 Tennis courts
1.6 Covered pavilions
1.5 Aquatics/pools

Extrapolating these figures to all NIRSA member colleges resulted in the following total number of units within all NIRSA member colleges:

868 Basketball courts
4,851 Tennis courts
1,890 Covered pavilions
210 Aquatics/pools

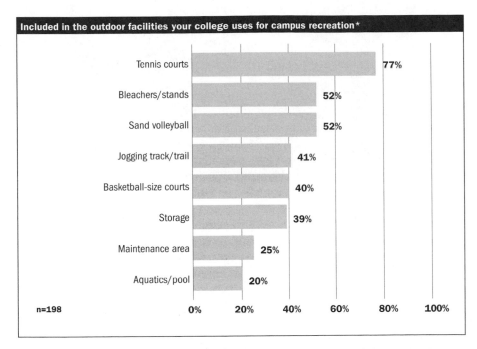

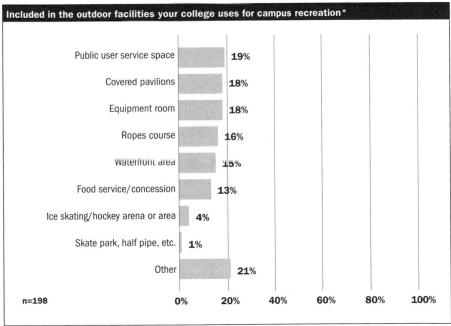

*Full text of the question: What is included in the outdoor facilities your college uses for campus recreation?

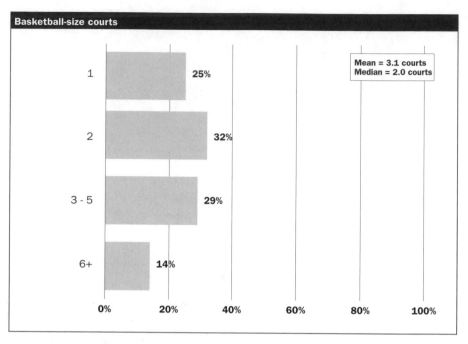

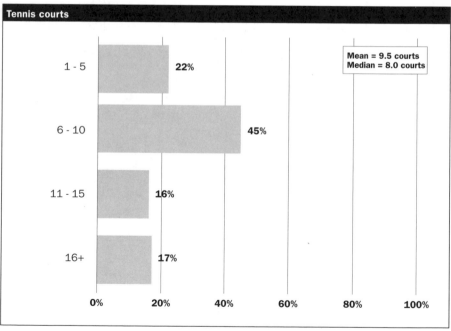

*Full text of the question: What is included in the outdoor facilities your college uses for campus recreation?

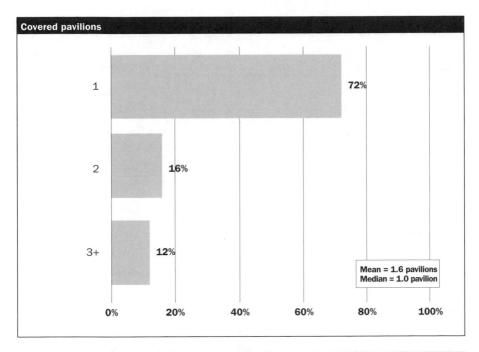

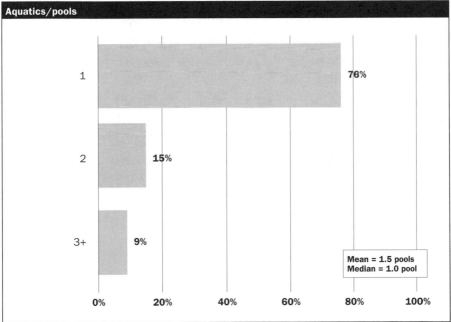

*Full text of the question: What is included in the outdoor facilities your college uses for campus recreation?

Planned Recreational Facilities

Campus Recreation Directors were requested to indicate what indoor and outdoor recreational facilities their colleges have planned to build or renovate within the next five (5) years. They were also requested to indicate approximated cost, year to be completed, whether it represented new construction or a renovation and to list square footage for indoor facilities, and the total lighted number of fields for outdoor facilities.

Planned Indoor Recreational Facilities

NIRSA member colleges in the study are planning to build or renovate 113 indoor recreational facilities within the next five years. One-in-six (16%) of these facilities will be completed this year while 1% will not be completed until 2008. Extrapolating results of this study to all NIRSA member colleges translated into 400 new or renovated indoor recreational facilities that will be constructed by NIRSA member colleges.

Project costs for new construction and renovations of indoor recreational facilities during the next five years ranged from $18,200 to $53,000,000. The typical (50th percentile) indoor recreational facility will cost $7,300,000, while the average project cost will be $10,994,000. Translating the figures in this study to all new construction and renovation projects for NIRSA member colleges resulted in $4.4 billion in project costs.

The project cost for the typical **renovation** over the next five years will be $1,500,000, while the project cost for typical **new construction** over the next five years will be $10,050,000. Average costs for renovations and new construction are estimated to be $8,398,343 and $12,656,719, respectively.

Median project costs for small, large and all colleges are shown below.

$7,300,000 All colleges
$12,000,000 Large colleges
$2,500,000 Small colleges

Renovation vs. New Construction. Based on the NIRSA member colleges in this study, three out of five facilities (60%) planned for the next five years will be new construction. Large colleges (55%) were about as likely as small ones (57%) to report that new construction (as opposed to renovations) is planned.

Cost per square foot of planned new construction is estimated to be $170, while cost per square foot for renovations to be completed over the next five years will be $90.

Description of Building/Renovation Projects. A plurality of colleges (34%) planned to construct or renovate a recreational center in the next five years. Three-in-ten colleges (29%) planned an addition or renovation to a specific indoor recreational sports building. One-in-eight colleges (12%) planned to add a fitness center, while 10% planned to add an aquatics center/pool.

Gross Square Footage. Gross square footage of indoor recreational facilities to be completed over the next five years ranged from 1,000 to 340,000. The typical (50th percentile) indoor recreational facility planned will have 42,000 square feet and the average facility will have 72,000 square feet. One-in-four indoor recreational facilities (25%) planned will have fewer than 10,000 square feet, while one-in-four will also have over 102,000 square feet. Median (50th percentile) square footage for indoor recreational facilities planned at small, large and all colleges are shown below:

42,000   All colleges
20,000   Small colleges
75,000   Large colleges

Translating the results of this study to all NIRSA member colleges will mean 28.8 million new square feet of indoor recreational facilities being built or renovated in the next five years.

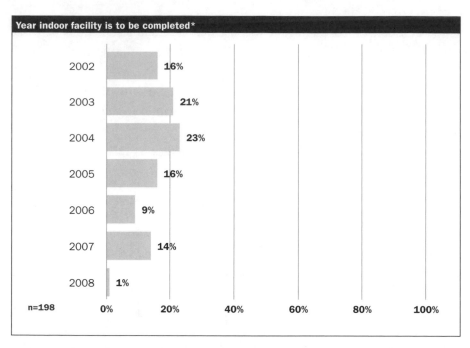

Year indoor facility is to be completed*

2002	16%
2003	21%
2004	23%
2005	16%
2006	9%
2007	14%
2008	1%

n=198   0%   20%   40%   60%   80%   100%

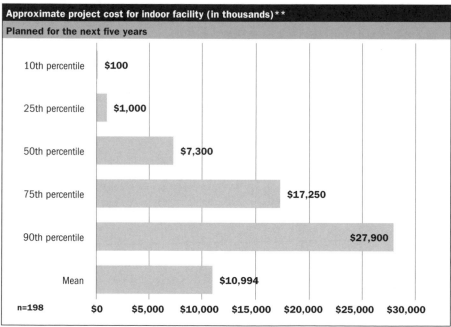

Approximate project cost for indoor facility (in thousands)**
Planned for the next five years

10th percentile	$100
25th percentile	$1,000
50th percentile	$7,300
75th percentile	$17,250
90th percentile	$27,900
Mean	$10,994

n=198 $0 $5,000 $10,000 $15,000 $20,000 $25,000 $30,000

*Full text of the question: This question is for campus recreational facilities planned on your campus for completion within the next five years. Please write the year the facilities will be built or renovated.
**Full text of the question: This question is for campus recreational facilities planned on your campus for completion within the next five years. Write down the approximate cost of the construction or renovation. You may use a range (e.g., $3 to $3.5 million) if you do not have specific numbers.

Indoor facilities – new or renovation*
Planned for the next five years

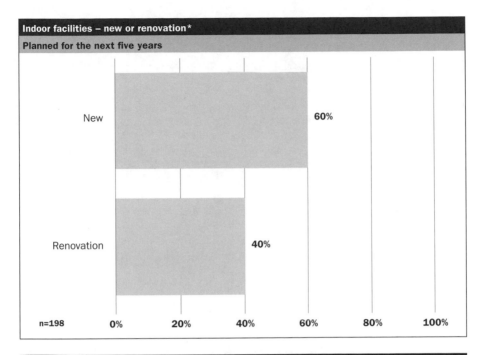

n=198

Planned indoor facility descriptions**
(Some descriptions contained multiple uses/facilities)

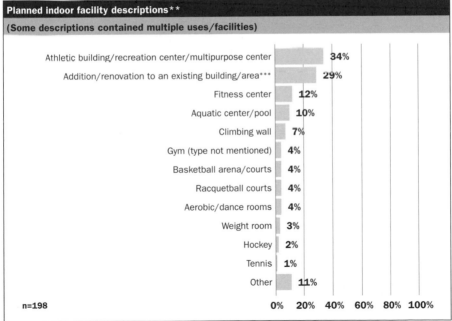

n=198

* Full text of the question: This question is for campus recreational facilities planned on your campus for completion within the next five years. Write an "N" or "R" if you are referencing New construction or Renovation.
** A complete list of the descriptions can be found in the Appendix.
***The description specified that the project was a renovation or addition to an existing facility.

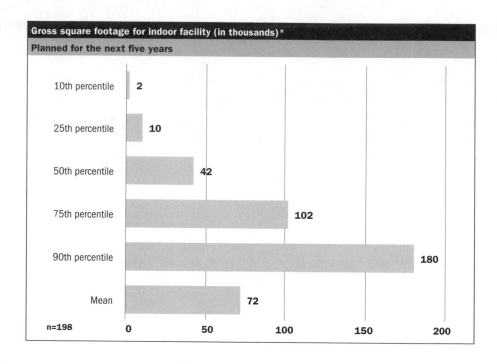

Gross square footage for indoor facility (in thousands) *

Planned for the next five years

Percentile	Value
10th percentile	2
25th percentile	10
50th percentile	42
75th percentile	102
90th percentile	180
Mean	72

n=198

* Full text of the question: This question is for campus recreational facilities planned on your campus for completion within the next five years. Write down the gross square footage for each indoor facility.

Components of Indoor Facilities

Graphs on pages 146-147 show the percentages of colleges that have specific components within their indoor recreational centers/complexes that are planned to be built or renovated over the next five years. More than one in three colleges will add or refurbish a cardiovascular area (35%) or free weights/circuit weight training area (34%). Within the next five years, three-in-ten colleges (30%) plan to add or refurbish office space, while nearly as many colleges (29%) plan to add or refurbish multipurpose rooms. About one-in-four colleges plan to add or refurbish basketball size courts (27%), storage (27%), locker rooms (26%), meeting space (26%), and equipment rooms (24%). Climbing walls, which only 32% of colleges now have, will be added or refurbished by 22% of colleges over the next five years.

Comparatively few colleges will add or refurbish the following within their indoor recreational centers/complexes:

- 6% Child care area
- 4% Inline sports arena
- 1% Ice skating/hockey arena or area
- 1% Bowling alley

These four components are also the ones that colleges are least likely to have within their indoor recreational facilities presently.

Components of Indoor Facilities by Size of College

The table on the page 145 compares the percentages of small and large colleges that have various components within their indoor recreational facilities.

As expected, larger colleges were more likely to have additions or refurbishing planned in more indoor recreational facilities than smaller colleges. There were exceptions: neither larger nor smaller colleges planned to add or refurbish ice skating/hockey skating arenas or bowling alleys, and larger and smaller colleges were equally likely to plan additions or refurbishing of game rooms.

For certain components such as basketball courts, Campus Recreational Directors were requested to indicate the number that were planned to be built or renovated within their indoor recreational centers/complexes over the next five years. The following are the average numbers:

4.2 Basketball courts
5.7 Racquetball/squash courts
2.8 Multipurpose rooms
1.2 Climbing walls
1.6 Aquatics/pools
1.1 Game rooms

Across all NIRSA member colleges, these numbers translated into the following total number of units:

794 Basketball courts
523 Racquetball/squash courts
574 Multipurpose rooms
182 Climbing walls
170 Aquatics/pools
70 Game rooms

Indoor recreational components	All Colleges	Small Colleges	Large Colleges
Cardiovascular fitness areas	35%	17%	66%
Free weights/circuit weight training	34%	17%	62%
Office space	30%	14%	55%
Multipurpose rooms	29%	12%	59%
Basketball-size courts	27%	12%	48%
Storage	27%	14%	59%
Locker rooms	26%	17%	45%
Meeting space	26%	14%	48%
Equipment rooms	24%	14%	48%
Maintenance area	23%	12%	55%
Climbing walls	22%	5%	45%
Classrooms	19%	12%	31%
Laundry room	19%	10%	38%
Food service	18%	10%	45%
First Aid/training room	17%	14%	24%
Jogging track (indoor)	17%	10%	38%
Aquatics/pools	15%	7%	28%
Racquetball/squash courts	13%	7%	28%
Outdoor pursuit center	11%	2%	24%
Soccer/floor hockey area	10%	0%	21%
Game rooms	9%	10%	10%
Sauna/steam room	7%	5%	17%
Child care area	6%	5%	10%
Inline sports arena	4%	0%	7%
Bowling alley	1%	0%	0%
Ice skating/hockey arena or area	1%	0%	0%

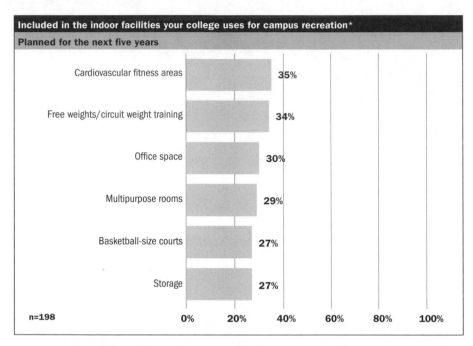

Included in the indoor facilities your college uses for campus recreation*

Planned for the next five years

- Cardiovascular fitness areas — 35%
- Free weights/circuit weight training — 34%
- Office space — 30%
- Multipurpose rooms — 29%
- Basketball-size courts — 27%
- Storage — 27%

n=198

0% 20% 40% 60% 80% 100%

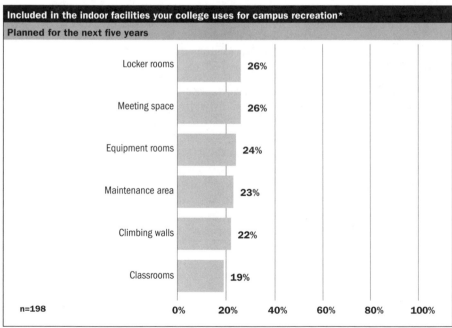

Included in the indoor facilities your college uses for campus recreation*

Planned for the next five years

- Locker rooms — 26%
- Meeting space — 26%
- Equipment rooms — 24%
- Maintenance area — 23%
- Climbing walls — 22%
- Classrooms — 19%

n=198

0% 20% 40% 60% 80% 100%

*Full text of the question: For indoor campus recreational facilities planned on your campus for completion within the next five years, please check what will be included in the construction and renovation of your campus' future student recreational facilities.

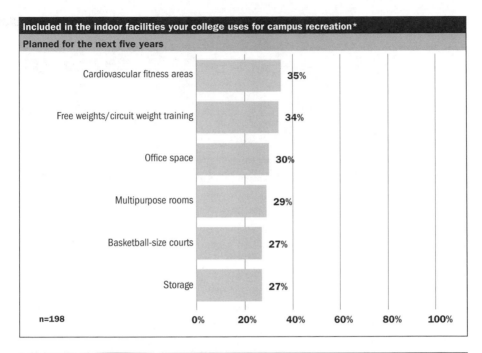

Included in the indoor facilities your college uses for campus recreation*

Planned for the next five years

Facility	Percent
Cardiovascular fitness areas	35%
Free weights/circuit weight training	34%
Office space	30%
Multipurpose rooms	29%
Basketball-size courts	27%
Storage	27%

n=198

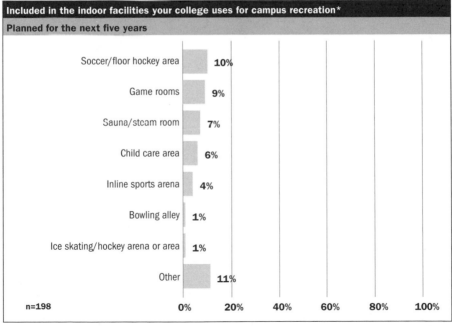

Included in the indoor facilities your college uses for campus recreation*

Planned for the next five years

Facility	Percent
Soccer/floor hockey area	10%
Game rooms	9%
Sauna/steam room	7%
Child care area	6%
Inline sports arena	4%
Bowling alley	1%
Ice skating/hockey arena or area	1%
Other	11%

n=198

*Full text of the question: For indoor campus recreational facilities planned on your campus for completion within the next five years, please check what will be included in the construction and renovation of your campus' future student recreational facilities.

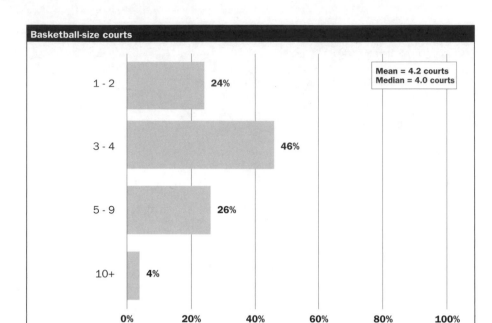

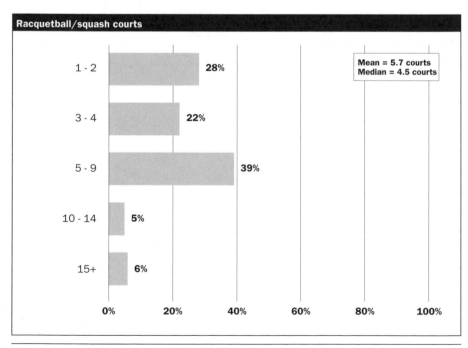

Note: No information was reported for bowling alleys.

Multipurpose rooms

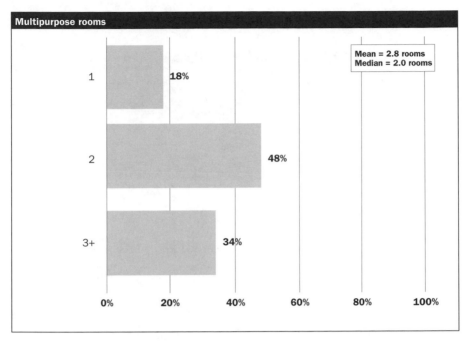

Mean = 2.8 rooms
Median = 2.0 rooms

1 — 18%
2 — 48%
3+ — 34%

Climbing walls

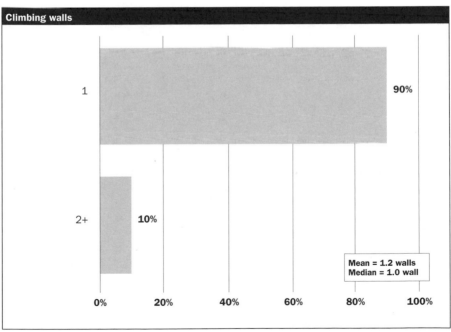

1 — 90%
2+ — 10%

Mean = 1.2 walls
Median = 1.0 wall

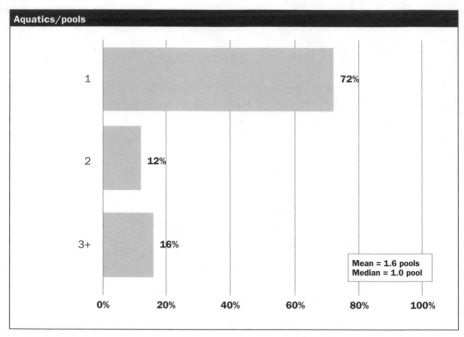

Aquatics/pools

- 1 — 72%
- 2 — 12%
- 3+ — 16%

Mean = 1.6 pools
Median = 1.0 pool

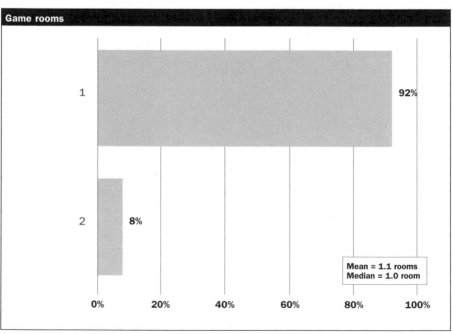

Game rooms

- 1 — 92%
- 2 — 8%

Mean = 1.1 rooms
Median = 1.0 room

Planned Outdoor Recreational Facilities

In the next five years, NIRSA member colleges in the study are planning to build or renovate 90 outdoor recreational facilities. Nearly seven out of ten (69%) will be new construction. One out of six of these new or renovated outdoor facilities (17%) were completed in 2002, while 15% will not be completed until 2007. Translating the findings from this study to all NIRSA member colleges resulted in 318 outdoor recreational projects planned by all NIRSA member colleges.

The typical (50th percentile) outdoor recreational project planned will cost $900,000 while the average project cost will be $1,743,000. The average is greater than the median because some projects will be very costly.

The average cost of new construction of outdoor recreational facilities will be $1,553,314 while the average cost of a renovation will be $2,136,173. Total project costs for the planned **new construction** of outdoor recreational facilities by NIRSA member colleges is $340,828,200, while total project costs for the planned **renovations** of outdoor recreational facilities is $210,583,900. Total project costs for all renovations and new construction of outdoor recreational facilities by NIRSA member firms is $551,412,100.

There are 721 flag football-size fields planned by NIRSA member firms over the next five years; 580 of the new fields will be lighted.

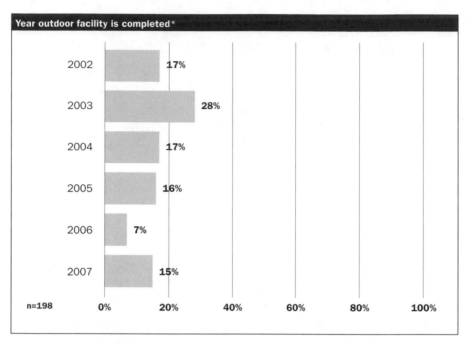

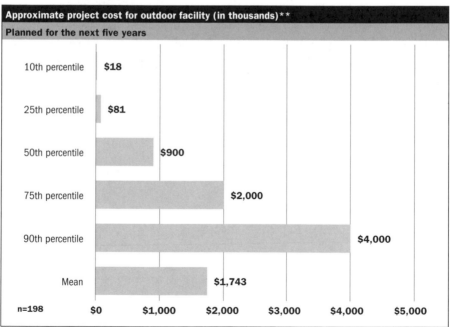

---

*Full text of the question: This question is for campus recreational facilities planned on your campus for completion within the next five years. Write the year the facilities will be built or renovated.

**Full text of the question: This question is for campus recreational facilities planned on your campus for completion within the next five years. Write down the approximate cost of the construction or renovation. You may use a range (e.g., $3 to $3.5 million) if you do not have specific numbers.

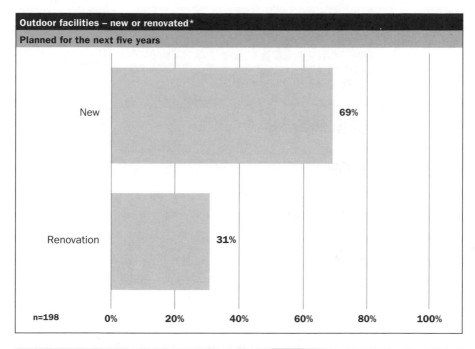

Outdoor facilities – new or renovated*

Planned for the next five years

New — 69%

Renovation — 31%

n=198

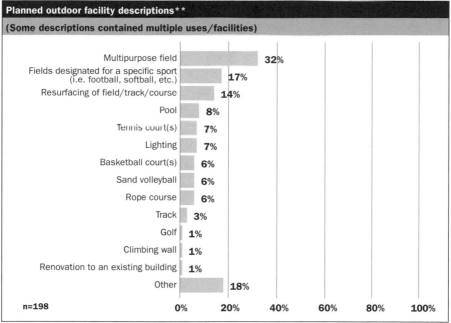

Planned outdoor facility descriptions**

(Some descriptions contained multiple uses/facilities)

Multipurpose field — 32%
Fields designated for a specific sport (i.e. football, softball, etc.) — 17%
Resurfacing of field/track/course — 14%
Pool — 8%
Tennis court(s) — 7%
Lighting — 7%
Basketball court(s) — 6%
Sand volleyball — 6%
Rope course — 6%
Track — 3%
Golf — 1%
Climbing wall — 1%
Renovation to an existing building — 1%
Other — 18%

n=198

*Full text of the question: This question is for campus recreational facilities planned on your campus for completion within the next five years. Write an "N" or "R" if you are referencing New construction or Renovation.
**A complete list of the descriptions can be found in the Appendix.

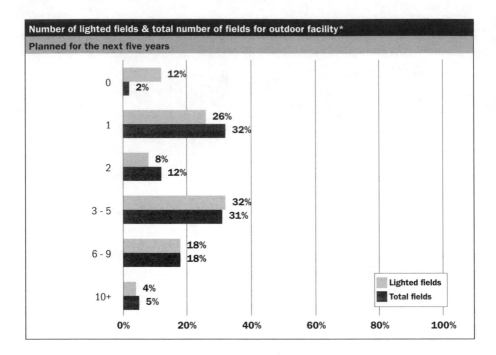

Number of lighted fields & total number of fields for outdoor facility*
Planned for the next five years

*Full text of the question: This question is for campus recreational facilities planned on your campus for completion within the next five years. Write in the number of lighted and total number of a flag football sized fields for each outdoor facility.

Components of Planned Outdoor Facilities

The graphs on page 157 show what percentages of colleges have various components planned for their outdoor recreational facilities over the next five years. Campus Recreation Directors indicated they planned to spend more on auxiliary projects rather than on playing fields. One-in-ten colleges planned to build or refurbish bleachers/stands (11%), storage (10%) and covered pavilions (10%). Nearly as many colleges planned to build or refurbish basketball-size courts (9%), jogging tracks/trails (9%), and sand volleyball (9%). As the percentages below demonstrate, larger colleges were more likely than smaller colleges to add each component to their outdoor recreational facilities.

For certain components such as basketball courts, Campus Recreational Directors were requested to indicate the number that were planned for their outdoor recreational facilities. The following are the average numbers:

2.4 Basketball courts
7.2 Tennis courts
1.1 Covered pavilions
1.2 Aquatics/pools

Extrapolating these figures to all NIRSA member colleges resulted in the following total number of outdoor recreational units planned for the next five years across all NIRSA member colleges:

144 Basketball courts
408 Tennis courts
 74 Covered pavilions
 55 Aquatics/pools

Outdoor recreational components	All Colleges	Small Colleges	Large Colleges
Bleachers/stands	11%	10%	14%
Covered pavilions	10%	5%	14%
Storage	10%	5%	21%
Basketball-size courts	9%	5%	14%
Jogging track/trail	9%	7%	14%
Sand volleyball	9%	2%	17%
Tennis courts	8%	2%	10%
Maintenance area	8%	2%	14%
Aquatics/pools	7%	0%	17%
Equipment room	7%	0%	10%
Public user service space	6%	2%	7%
Food service/concession	6%	2%	10%
Ropes course	6%	0%	7%
Waterfront area	3%	0%	7%
Skate park, half pipe, etc.	3%	2%	3%
Ice skating/hockey arena or area	2%	0%	3%

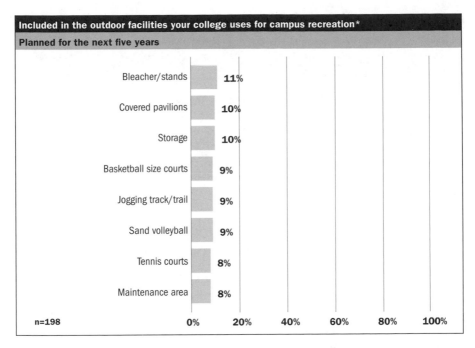

Included in the outdoor facilities your college uses for campus recreation*

Planned for the next five years

Facility	Percentage
Bleacher/stands	11%
Covered pavilions	10%
Storage	10%
Basketball size courts	9%
Jogging track/trail	9%
Sand volleyball	9%
Tennis courts	8%
Maintenance area	8%

n=198

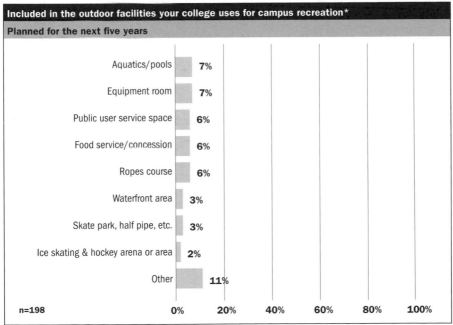

Included in the outdoor facilities your college uses for campus recreation*

Planned for the next five years

Facility	Percentage
Aquatics/pools	7%
Equipment room	7%
Public user service space	6%
Food service/concession	6%
Ropes course	6%
Waterfront area	3%
Skate park, half pipe, etc.	3%
Ice skating & hockey arena or area	2%
Other	11%

n=198

*Full text of the question: For outdoor campus recreational facilities planned on your campus for completion within the next five years, please check what will be included in the construction and renovation of your campus' future student recreational facilities.

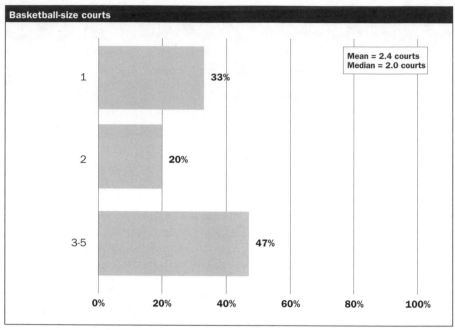

Basketball-size courts

Mean = 2.4 courts
Median = 2.0 courts

1 — 33%
2 — 20%
3-5 — 47%

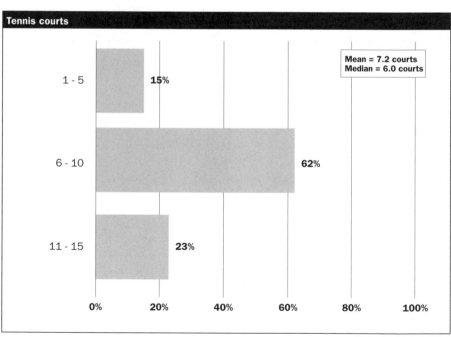

Tennis courts

Mean = 7.2 courts
Median = 6.0 courts

1 - 5 — 15%
6 - 10 — 62%
11 - 15 — 23%

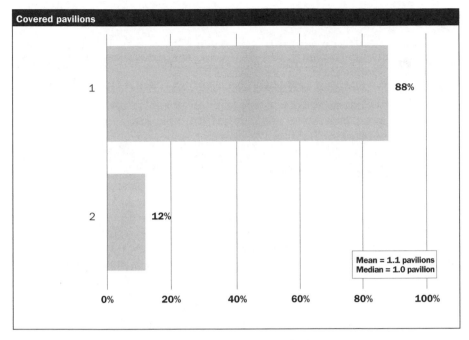

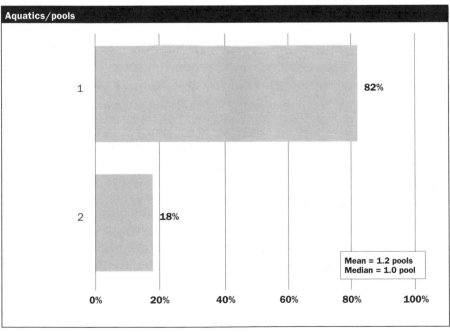

Annual Expenditures

Campus Recreation Directors were given a list of expense categories and requested to indicate how much their colleges had spent in each category during the most recent fiscal year. Expenditures were grouped into the following categories:

- Recreational sporting equipment
- Facilities operations
- Administration
- Miscellaneous

There were several expense items within each of these broad categories. The table on page 162 shows mean (average) and median (50th percentile) expenditures for each category along with 10th, 25th, 75th and 90th percentiles.

Percentiles are interpreted in the following manner. From the table on page 162, the 10th percentile for game/sports equipment was $500. That means that 90% of the colleges spent more than $500 on game/sports equipment in their most recent fiscal year. Likewise, the 90th percentile for game/sports equipment is $25,000. This means that only 10% of colleges spent more than $25,000 in their most recent fiscal year on game/sports equipment; conversely, 90% of colleges spent less than $25,000 on game/sports equipment.

When interpreting expenditures in the table on page 162, it should be noted that the "typical" college is represented by the 50th percentile (median) figures. For example, the typical college spent $3,000 on game/sports equipment, $2,000 on goals, nets, mats, pads, and the typical college spent $3,000 on apparel.

When translating expenditures in the table on page 162 from this sample of colleges to all NIRSA member colleges, the mean (average) figures should be used. The average expenditure for game/sports equipment was $10,715; for goals, nets, mats, pads it was $3,928, etc.

Extrapolating average expenditures from the table on page 162 to all NIRSA member colleges resulted in the annual expenditures for all NIRSA member colleges shown on page 161.

Total Annual Expenditures by All NIRSA Member Colleges

Recreational Sporting Equipment

Game/Sports Equipment $7,500,500

Goals, Nets, Mats, Pads, Etc. $2,749,600

Apparel $3,989,300

Outdoor Recreation Equipment $5,226,900

Other Recreational Sporting Equipment $1,567,000

Facilities Operations

Video/Audio/Entertainment Systems, Cardio Theater, Etc. $4,919,600

First Aid, Medical Supplies $1,320,900

Utilities $142,171,400

General Maintenance and Janitorial Supplies $39,978,400

Floor Maintenance, Resealing, Surfaces, Carpeting, Etc. $10,612,000

Field Maintenance, Fences, Backstops, Goals,
Landscaping, Etc. $13,022,800

Safety And Security.. $5,643,400

Facility Components $7,896,700

Other Facilities Operations $8,146,100

Administration

Computers/Software/Technical $17,707,200

Marketing/Promotions/Incentives................................. $8,281,000

Office Supplies/Equipment.. $7,263,200

Consultants/Contractual Services $11,930,800

Salaries And Wages $337,827,000

Dues, Memberships, Publications $1,493,800

Other Administration $11,700,500

Miscellaneous

Appliances/furniture $8,371,300

Child care facilities/services $140,000

Travel $8,787,800

Other miscellaneous $123,369,400

Expenditures During Most Recent Fiscal Year						
			PERCENTILES			
EXPENSE CATEGORIES	10th	25th	50th	75th	90TH	MEAN
Recreational sporting equipment						
Game/sports equipment	$500	$1,200	$3,000	$10,000	$25,000	$10,715
Goals, nets, mats, pads, etc	$200	$556	$2,000	$5,000	$10,000	$3,928
Apparel	$400	$1,500	$3,000	$6,000	$14,700	$5,699
Outdoor recreation equipment	$0	$500	$2,000	$5,000	$20,000	$7,467
Other recreational sporting equipment*	$700	$2,500	$5,000	$30,000	$66,532	$19,445
Facilities operations						
Video/audio/entertainment systems, cardio theater, etc.	$0	$350	$2,000	$5,000	$10,000	$7,028
First aid, medical supplies	$100	$288	$800	$2,000	$5,000	$1,887
Utilities	$0	$9,000	$114,600	$300,000	$552,000	$203,102
General maintenance and janitorial supplies	$440	$3,000	$20,000	$55,486	$125,000	$57,112
Floor maintenance, resealing surfaces, carpeting, etc.	$800	$2,800	$10,000	$19,533	$39,000	$15,160
Field maintenance, fences, backstops, goals, landscaping, etc.	$18	$1,000	$4,500	$18,125	$50,000	$18,604
Safety and security	$0	$1,000	$2,500	$10,000	$20,000	$8,062
Facility components	$0	$500	$2,000	$5,750	$24,500	$11,281
Other facilities operations**	$1,180	$3,185	$9,488	$76,750	$194,000	$82,301
Administration						
Computers/software/technical	$360	$1,500	$5,000	$12,000	$26,560	$25,296
Marketing/promotions/incentives	$275	$1,000	$3,000	$9,000	$24,255	$11,830
Office supplies/equipment	$300	$800	$2,500	$10,000	$29,800	$10,376
Consultants/contractual Services	$0	$325	$5,500	$15,000	$47,470	$17,044
Salaries and wages	$18,400	$68,000	$200,000	$700,000	$1,200,000	$482,610
Dues, memberships, Publications	$300	$500	$1,000	$2,000	$4,000	$2,134
Other administration***	$1,400	$4,450	$17,000	$85,000	$560,000	$116,078
Miscellaneous						
Appliances/furniture	$0	$350	$2,000	$6,000	$25,000	$11,959
Child care facilities/services	$0	$0	$0	$0	$0	$200
Travel	$500	$1,725	$5,000	$11,461	$32,610	$12,554
Other miscellaneous****	$960	$4,200	$10,000	$16,000	$1,481,240	$176,242

*Figures were from only 23 colleges
**Figures were from only 28 colleges
***Figures were from only 29 colleges
****Figures were from only 11 colleges

Expenditures By College Size

The table below shows median (50th percentile) expenditures by college size. As expected, larger colleges' median expenditures exceed those for smaller colleges in all areas.

Expenditures During Most Recent Fiscal Year by College Size			
	MEDIAN EXPENDITURES		
EXPENSE CATEGORIES	ALL COLLEGES	SMALL COLLEGES	LARGE COLLEGES
Recreational Sporting Equipment			
Game/Sports Equipment	$3,000	$1,750	$10,500
Goals, Nets, Mats, Pads, Etc.	$2,000	$1,000	$5,000
Apparel	$3,000	$1,500	$7,750
Outdoor Recreation Equipment	$2,000	$500	$8,000
Facilities Operations			
Video/Audio/Entertainment Systems, Cardio Theater, Etc.	$2,000	$700	$2,000
First Aid, Medical Supplies	$800	$450	$2,000
Utilities	$114,600	$18,000	$255,000
General Maintenance And Janitorial Supplies	$20,000	$2,800	$35,442
Floor Maintenance, Resealing Surfaces, Carpeting, Etc.	$10,000	$3,000	$20,000
Field Maintenance, Fences, Backstops, Goals, Landscaping, Etc.	$4,500	$500	$15,083
Safety And Security	$2,500	$900	$2,750
Facility Components	$2,000	$850	$2,750
Administration			
Computers/Software/Technical	$5,000	$500	$16,000
Marketing/Promotions/Incentives	$3,000	$750	$14,250
Office Supplies/Equipment	$2,500	$675	$13,750
Consultants/Contractual Services	$5,500	$1,400	$13,300
Salaries And Wages	$200,000	$50,000	$790,471
Dues, Memberships, Publications	$1,000	$500	$2,225
Miscellaneous			
Appliances/Furniture	$2,000	$300	$5,000
Child Care Facilities/Services	$0	$0	$0
Travel	$5,000	$1,090	$15,000

Infrequent Expenditures

Certain expenditures occur on a periodic basis over several years. Buying free weights or cardiovascular equipment fits this description. Campus Recreation Directors were requested to indicate how much they had spent over the past ten years on infrequently purchased items and how much they planned to spend over the next five years on these items.

Past Expenditures for Infrequently Purchased Items

The table below shows detailed expenditure information on items that were purchased infrequently over the past ten years. The top table on page 165 contains percentile information. For example, the 10th percentile for free weights expenditures was $3,600. This means that 10% of colleges in the study spent $3,600 or less on free weights over the past ten years. Conversely, the 90th percentile for free weights was $300,000 which means that 10% of colleges spent more than $300,000 on free weights over the past ten years.

The 50th percentile is normally considered a gauge for the "typical" college. For example, the typical college spent $70,000 on free weights over the past ten years. To determine total expenditures for all NIRSA member colleges, the average expenditure ($133,160 for free weights) would be multiplied by the total number of NIRSA member colleges.

Total expenditures by all NIRSA member colleges over the past ten years for infrequently purchased items are shown below:

Total Expenditures – Past 10 years	
Free weights/weight training circuit equipment	$93,212,000
Video/audio/entertainment systems, cardio theater, etc.	$12,261,200
Cardiovascular equipment	$89,786,200
Laundry and maintenance equipment	$19,876,500
Miscellaneous facility equipment (standards, goals, netting, padding, backboards, curtains, etc.)	$31,487,400
Resurfacing (courts, lanes, rooms, etc.)	$61,107,800
Architectural services	$94,275,720
Aquatics equipment	$24,761,800
Lighting	$108,398,500
Other infrequently purchased items	$12,867,400

Infrequent Expenditures Over the Past 10 Years						
	PERCENTILES					
EXPENSE CATEGORIES	10th	25th	50th	75th	90TH	MEAN
Free weights/weight training circuit equipment	$3,600	$15,000	$70,000	$150,000	$300,000	$133,160
Video/audio/entertainment systems, cardio theater, etc.	$580	$2,000	$6,500	$25,000	$50,000	$17,516
Cardiovascular equipment	$9,600	$25,000	$60,000	$200,000	$300,000	$128,266
Laundry & maintenance equipment	$500	$3,000	$10,000	$24,000	$50,000	$28,395
Misc. facility equipment	$2,000	$5,000	$10,000	$30,000	$96,000	$44,982
Resurfacing (courts, lanes, rooms, etc.)	$1,400	$10,000	$30,000	$100,000	$206,000	$87,297
Architectural services	$0	$5,000	$25,000	$400,000	$1,000,000	$336,699
Aquatics equipment	$300	$2,500	$10,000	$25,000	$74,000	$35,374
Lighting	$0	$1,600	$40,000	$156,000	$296,000	$154,855

Expenditures for Infrequently Purchased Items by College Size

The table below shows median expenditures over the past ten years for infrequently purchased items by size of college. As expected, median expenditures for larger colleges greatly exceed expenditures for smaller colleges. In many cases, expenditures by larger colleges exceed those of smaller colleges by huge multiples (e.g., $100,000 for aquatics for larger colleges vs. $1,600 for smaller colleges).

Infrequent Expenditures Over the Past 10 Years			
	MEDIAN EXPENDITURES		
EXPENSE CATEGORIES	ALL COLLEGES	SMALL COLLEGES	LARGE COLLEGES
Free Weights/Weight Training Circuit Equipment	$70,000	$30,000	$175,000
Video/Audio/Entertainment Systems, Cardio Theater, Etc.	$6,500	$5,000	$10,000
Cardiovascular Equipment	$60,000	$25,000	$250,000
Laundry & Maintenance Equipment	$10,000	$5,000	$16,000
Misc. Facility Equipment	$10,000	$6,000	$20,000
Resurfacing (Courts, Lanes, Rooms, Etc.)	$30,000	$10,500	$100,000
Architectural Services	$25,000	$5,500	$200,000
Aquatics Equipment	$10,000	$1,000	$17,500
Lighting	$40,000	$1,600	$100,000

Future Expenditures for Infrequently Purchased Items

The top table on page 167 shows detailed expenditure information on items that will be purchased infrequently over the next five years, and contains percentile information. For example, the 10th percentile for free weights expenditures was $4,000. This means that 10% of colleges in the study will spend $4,000 or less on free weights. Conversely, the 90th percentile for free weights was $200,000 which means that 10% of colleges will spend more than $200,000 on free weights.

The 50th percentile is normally considered a gauge for the "typical" college. For example, the typical college will spend $29,500 on free weights. To determine total expenditures for all NIRSA member colleges, the average expenditure ($84,079 for free weights) would be multiplied by the total number of NIRSA member colleges.

Total expenditures by all NIRSA member colleges over the next five years for infrequently purchased items are shown below:

Total Expenditures — Next 5 years	
Free Weights/Weight Training Circuit Equipment	$58,855,300
Video/Audio/Entertainment Systems, Cardio Theater, Etc.	$12,741,400
Cardiovascular Equipment	$81,855,900
Laundry And Maintenance Equipment	$13,427,400
Miscellaneous Facility Equipment (Standards, Goals, Netting, Padding, Backboards, Curtains, Etc.)	$17,325,000
Resurfacing (Courts, Lanes, Rooms, Etc.)	$41,867,000
Architectural Services	$66,348,000
Aquatics Equipment	$20,711,600
Lighting	$99,675,100
Other Infrequently Purchased Items	$22,445,486

Expenditures for Infrequently Purchased Items by College Size

The table on the bottom of page 167 shows estimated median expenditures over the next five years for infrequently purchased items by size of college. As expected, median expenditures for larger colleges are expected to greatly exceed expenditures for smaller colleges. In many cases, expenditures by larger colleges are expected to exceed those of smaller colleges by huge multiples (e.g. $500,000 for aquatics for larger colleges vs. $10,000 for smaller colleges).

Infrequent Expenditures Over the Next 5 Years

	PERCENTILES					
EXPENSE CATEGORIES	10th	25th	50th	75th	90TH	MEAN
Free weights/weight training circuit equipment	$4,000	$10,000	$29,500	$100,000	$200,000	$84,079
Video/audio/entertainment systems, cardio theater, etc.	$1,000	$2,625	$10,000	$21,875	$50,000	$18,202
Cardiovascular equipment	$10,000	$20,000	$50,000	$150,000	$300,000	$116,937
Laundry and maintenance Equipment	$0	$2,750	$10,000	$21,000	$40,000	$19,182
Miscellaneous facility equipment	$700	$3,000	$10,000	$25,000	$50,000	$24,750
Resurfacing (courts, lanes, rooms, etc.)	$2,450	$10,000	$27,500	$60,000	$120,400	$59,810
Architectural services	$0	$2,500	$25,000	$175,000	$940,000	$243,033
Aquatics equipment	$300	$3,000	$10,000	$25,000	$80,000	$29,588
Lighting	$0	$600	$20,000	$102,500	$250,000	$142,393

Infrequent Expenditures Over the Next 5 Years

	MEDIAN EXPENDITURES		
EXPENSE CATEGORIES	ALL COLLEGES	SMALL COLLEGES	LARGE COLLEGES
Free weights/weight training circuit equipment	$10,000	$29,500	$75,000
Video/audio/entertainment systems, cardio theater, etc.	$2,750	$10,000	$15,000
Cardiovascular equipment	$12,250	$50,000	$200,000
Laundry and maintenance equipment	$3,500	$10,000	$20,000
Miscellaneous facility equipment	$4,000	$10,000	$30,000
Resurfacing (courts, lanes, rooms, etc.)	$10,000	$27,500	$57,500
Architectural services	$0	$25,000	$100,000
Aquatics equipment	$1,000	$10,000	$500,000
Lighting	$1,000	$20,000	$57,500

Food service

Not quite half of the colleges in the study (46%) had food service operations as part of their campus recreation facilities. Most college recreation departments that did get involved in food service outsourced all of their food service activities. Only one-in-25 colleges (4%) handled all of their food service internally within the recreational sports area.

Keeping in mind that a majority of colleges did **not** have food service as part of the recreational sports department, the figures in the graphs on page 170-171 demonstrate food service revenue received from direct sales and from firms to which the food service operations were outsourced. Average and median (50th percentile) revenue from outsourcing and direct sales for smaller and larger colleges is shown below.

Food Service Revenue	REVENUE FROM OUTSOURCING	REVENUE FROM DIRECT SALES
All colleges		
Average	$6,008	$16,336
Median (50th percentile)	$0	$0
Large colleges		
Average	$13,363	$34,492
Median (50th percentile)	$15,000	$0
Small colleges		
Average	$944	$2,250
Median (50th percentile)	$0	$0

Food service Items

The table on page 169 shows the percentages of colleges that carry certain items as part of their food service operation. Soft drinks and bottled water led the list with about one-in-three colleges (32%) carrying these items. Chips, pretzels and other snacks (28%) and candy (26%) were the next most frequently carried items. Healthier items such as fresh fruit (15%) and salads (13%) were carried by fewer colleges.

College Recreation Directors were requested to indicate which food service items had the highest unit sales.

The listing below prioritizes food service items with respect to unit sales.

- Soft drinks
- Bottled water
- Fruit/health drinks, smoothies, etc.
- Sandwiches, wraps, etc.
- Health bars, energy bars
- Candy
- Chips, pretzels, etc.
- Coffee, tea, milk
- Fresh fruit
- Pizza, pasta, etc.
- Salads
- Soup, chili, etc.
- Ice cream, yogurt, etc.
- Breads, rolls, etc.

The percentages below show what percentages of colleges by size carried specific food service items. In general, larger colleges were more likely to carry food service items. Smaller colleges were equally likely to carry chips and pretzels and more likely than larger colleges to carry pizza and pasta.

Food Service Items			
		MEDIAN EXPENDITURES	
	ALL	SMALL	LARGE
EXPENSE CATEGORIES	COLLEGES	COLLEGES	COLLEGES
Soft drinks	32%	33%	41%
Bottled water	32%	31%	41%
Chips, pretzels, etc.	28%	31%	31%
Candy	26%	29%	28%
Fruit/health drinks, smoothies, etc.	22%	19%	35%
Health bars, energy bars, etc.	19%	14%	35%
Sandwiches, wraps, etc.	15%	14%	31%
Fresh fruit	15%	10%	28%
Coffee, tea, milk	15%	14%	28%
Salads	13%	12%	21%
Ice cream, yogurt, etc.	9%	10%	21%
Breads, rolls, etc.	9%	7%	17%
Soup, chili, etc.	8%	7%	14%
Pizza, pasta	7%	12%	7%

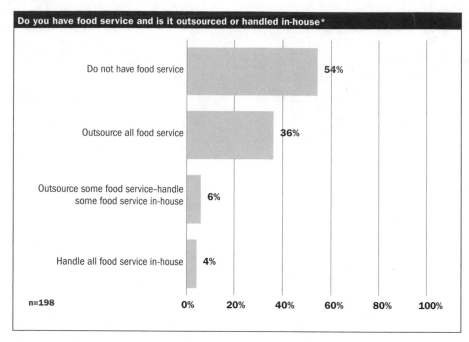

Do you have food service and is it outsourced or handled in-house*

- Do not have food service — 54%
- Outsource all food service — 36%
- Outsource some food service–handle some food service in-house — 6%
- Handle all food service in-house — 4%

n=198

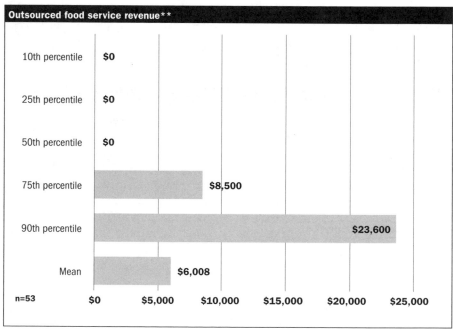

Outsourced food service revenue**

- 10th percentile — $0
- 25th percentile — $0
- 50th percentile — $0
- 75th percentile — $8,500
- 90th percentile — $23,600
- Mean — $6,008

n=53

*Full text of the question: Do you have food service (including vending machines) as part of your campus recreation, and if so, is it outsourced or handled in-house?

**Full text of the question: Please estimate The revenue your department received from outsourced food service in the past fiscal year.

Direct sales from in-house food service*

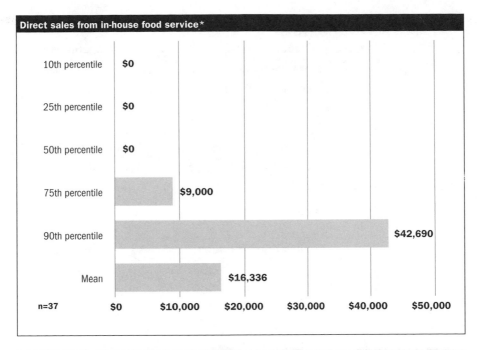

10th percentile	$0
25th percentile	$0
50th percentile	$0
75th percentile	$9,000
90th percentile	$42,690
Mean	$16,336

n=37 $0 $10,000 $20,000 $30,000 $40,000 $50,000

Items sold in food service operation**

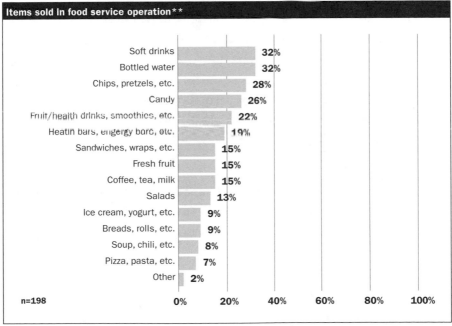

Soft drinks	32%
Bottled water	32%
Chips, pretzels, etc.	28%
Candy	26%
Fruit/health drinks, smoothies, etc.	22%
Health bars, energy bars, etc.	19%
Sandwiches, wraps, etc.	15%
Fresh fruit	15%
Coffee, tea, milk	15%
Salads	13%
Ice cream, yogurt, etc.	9%
Breads, rolls, etc.	9%
Soup, chili, etc.	8%
Pizza, pasta, etc.	7%
Other	2%

n=198   0%   20%   40%   60%   80%   100%

*Full text of the question: Please estimate The revenue your department received from in-house food service in the past fiscal year.
**Full text of the question: Please check the items you sell as part of your food service operation.

Recreational Sports Budgets

Campus Recreation Directors were asked to list their capital, operational and other budgets, as well as their total budgets. Graphs on pages 174-175 show percentiles and mean figures for these four budget components.

Capital Budget

Many colleges (21%) indicated that they had no capital budgets. The typical (50th percentile) college had a capital budget of $50,000, while the average capital budget was $540,000. Median and average capital budgets for smaller and larger colleges are shown below.

	Median capital budget	Average capital budget
Small colleges	$10,000	$26,600
Large colleges	$300,000	$1,385,600

Operational Budget

Operational budgets ranged from a few thousand dollars to more than seven million dollars. Some Campus Recreation Directors indicated that their expenditures were contained in other campus budgets. The typical college had an operational budget for campus recreation of $390,000, while the average operational budget was $862,000. Ten percent of colleges had operational budgets that exceeded $2.5 million. Median and average operational budgets for smaller and larger colleges are shown below.

	Median capital budget	Average capital budget
Small colleges	$30,000	$57,814
Large colleges	$1,715,000	$2,315,683

All Other Budgets

In addition to capital and operational budgets, colleges had significant monies allocated to "other" budgets. The typical college had $40,000 in other budgets, while the average amount in an "other" budget was $438,000. Median and average "other" budgets for smaller and larger colleges are shown below.

	Median capital budget	Average "other" budget
Small colleges	$5,000	$108,318
Large colleges	$250,000	$968,269

Total Budget

Total budgets ranged from a few thousand dollars to over twenty million dollars. The typical college had a total budget of $515,000, and the average total budget was $1,368,000. One in ten colleges in this study had total budgets in excess of $3,756,000 (90th percentile). Median and average total budgets for smaller and larger colleges are shown below.

	Median capital budget	Average total budget
Small colleges	$49,700	$131,715
Large colleges	$3,093,100	$4,160,729

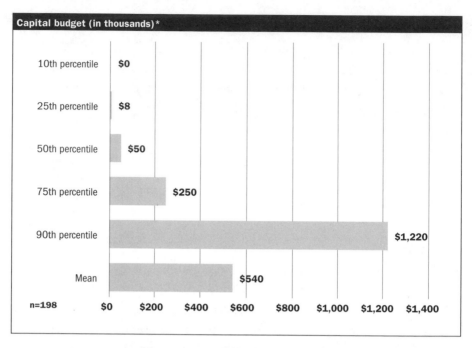

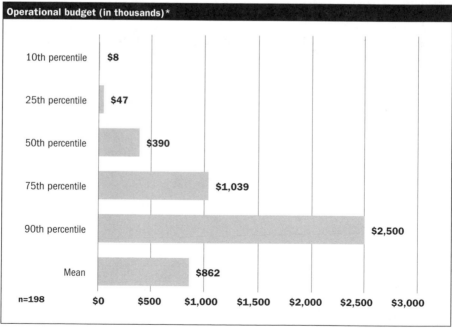

*Full text of the question: Please write in your college's total (capital and operational) budget this year for recreational sports. You can approximate or use ranges.

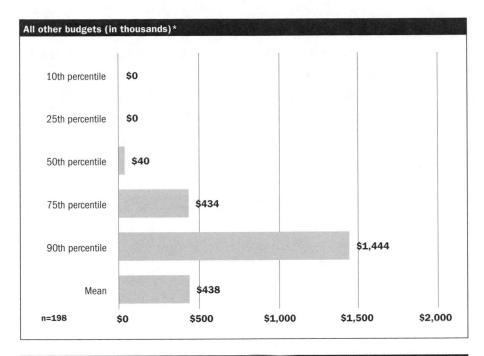

All other budgets (in thousands)*

- 10th percentile: $0
- 25th percentile: $0
- 50th percentile: $40
- 75th percentile: $434
- 90th percentile: $1,444
- Mean: $438

n=198

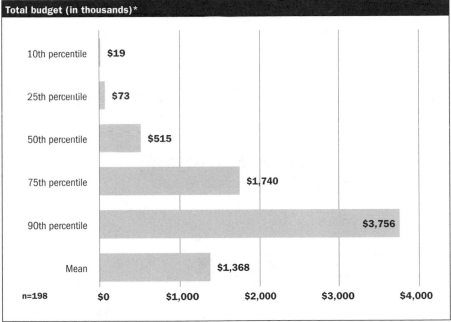

Total budget (in thousands)*

- 10th percentile: $19
- 25th percentile: $73
- 50th percentile: $515
- 75th percentile: $1,740
- 90th percentile: $3,756
- Mean: $1,368

n=198

*Full text of the question: Please write in your college's total (capital and operational) budget this year for recreational sports. You can approximate or use ranges.

Promotions

Not quite half of the colleges (45%) in the study allowed paid **outdoor** promotional signs and boards. Three out of five colleges (62%) permitted paid **indoor** promotional signs and boards. As the bottom graph below illustrates, smaller colleges were more likely to permit **outdoor** promotional signs and boards and larger colleges were more likely to permit **indoor** promotional signs and boards.

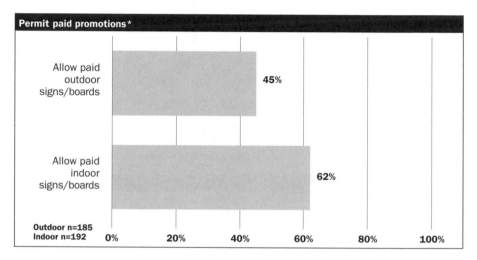

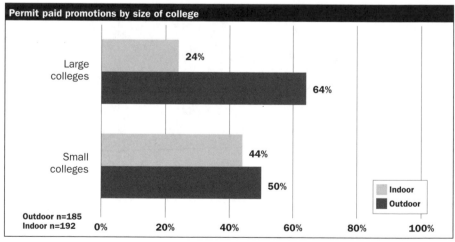

Purchasing Authority

More than nine out of ten colleges in the study had a Director of Recreational Sports position (91%) and exactly half of the colleges had an Assistant Director (50%). Two-in-five colleges had an Associate Director (40%) or a Coordinator (40%). One-in-six colleges (16%) had some other job position within the recreational sports area.

Nearly all Directors of Recreational Sports (98%) had purchasing authority. The Director at a typical college (50th percentile) had authority to purchase $5,000, while the average amount over which Directors had authority was $77,000.

Four out of five Associate Directors (81%) had purchasing authority with the typical Associate Director having authority to purchase $5,000. The average amount over which Associate Directors had authority to purchase was $47,400.

Nearly four out of five Assistant Directors (78%) had purchasing authority. The typical Assistant Director had authority to purchase $2,000, and the average amount of purchase authority for Assistant Directors was $5,700.

Three out of five Coordinators (63%) also had purchasing authority with the typical college assigning $2,500 worth of purchasing power to Coordinators. The average amount over which Coordinators had authority was $5,500.

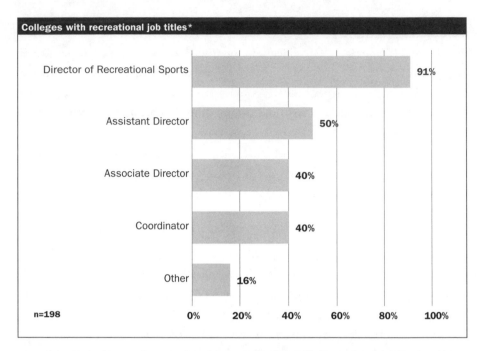

Colleges with recreational job titles*

- Director of Recreational Sports — 91%
- Assistant Director — 50%
- Associate Director — 40%
- Coordinator — 40%
- Other — 16%

n=198

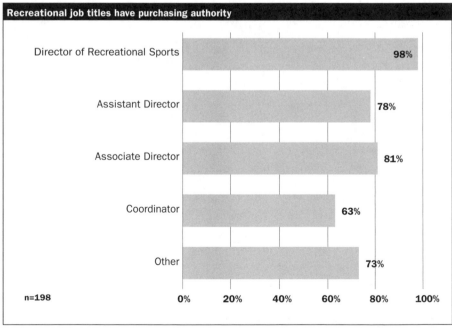

Recreational job titles have purchasing authority

- Director of Recreational Sports — 98%
- Assistant Director — 78%
- Associate Director — 81%
- Coordinator — 63%
- Other — 73%

n=198

*Full text of the question: Please check each job title/position that exists at your college. Check if each level has purchasing authority for your college's recreational sports purchases, and write in the maximum dollar amount of purchase over which this person has for a single purchase. (If "No Limit," please write NL).

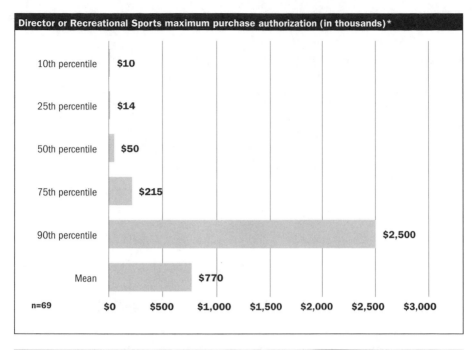

Director or Recreational Sports maximum purchase authorization (in thousands)*

Percentile	Value
10th percentile	$10
25th percentile	$14
50th percentile	$50
75th percentile	$215
90th percentile	$2,500
Mean	$770

n=69

$0 $500 $1,000 $1,500 $2,000 $2,500 $3,000

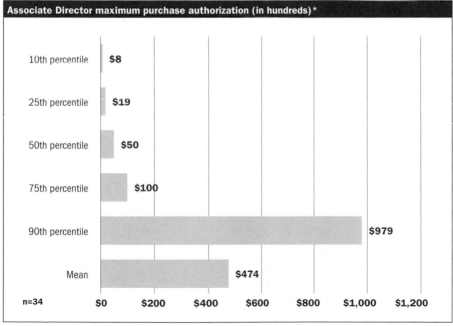

Associate Director maximum purchase authorization (in hundreds)*

Percentile	Value
10th percentile	$8
25th percentile	$19
50th percentile	$50
75th percentile	$100
90th percentile	$979
Mean	$474

n=34

$0 $200 $400 $600 $800 $1,000 $1,200

*Full text of the question: Please check each job title/position that exists at your college. Check if each level has purchasing authority for your college's recreational sports purchases, and write in the maximum dollar amount of purchase over which this person has for a single purchase. (If "No Limit," please write NL).

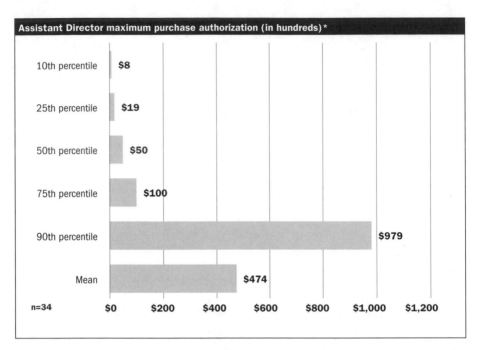

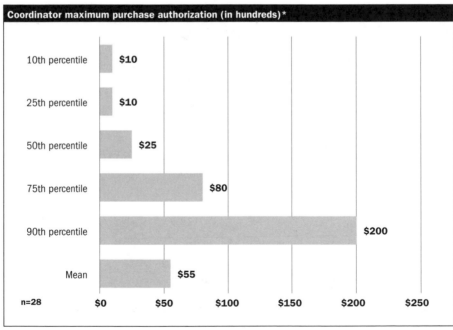

*Full text of the question: Please check each job title/position that exists at your college. Check if each level has purchasing authority for your college's recreational sports purchases, and write in the maximum dollar amount of purchase over which this person has for a single purchase. (If "No Limit," please write NL).

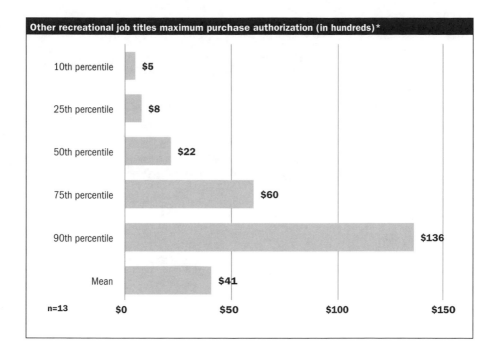

Other recreational job titles maximum purchase authorization (in hundreds)*

- 10th percentile: $5
- 25th percentile: $8
- 50th percentile: $22
- 75th percentile: $60
- 90th percentile: $136
- Mean: $41

n=13

$0 $50 $100 $150

*Full text of the question: Please check each job title/position that exists at your college. Check if each level has purchasing authority for your college's recreational sports purchases, and write in the maximum dollar amount of purchase over which this person has for a single purchase. (If "No Limit," please write NL).

Section III:

Buying Power of Recreational Sports Participants

Buying Power of Recreational Sports Participants

This study also assessed buying power of participants in recreational sports programs and activities through self-report measures of spending on a wide range of products and services during a 30-day period.

- Athletic apparel/clothes
- Athletic equipment
- Athletic shoes
- Restaurants
- Food (grocery stores, convenience stores, etc.)
- Cars (gas, repair, etc.)
- Clothes, shoes (excluding athletic clothes or athletic shoes)
- Soft drinks, sports drinks
- Personal care, toiletries
- Vitamins, health supplements, health food
- Bottled water
- Household items
- Videos, movies, DVDs, CDs, headsets, etc.
- Sporting events, concerts, clubs, etc.
- TVs, radios, stereos
- Computers, pagers, CD burners, PDAs, cell phones
- Travel/vacation
- Alcohol, cigarettes

To ease the reporting burden, students were given the following categories:

- $0
- $1 - $10
- $11 - $25
- $26 - $50
- $51 - $100
- $101 - $200
- $201 - $500
- More than $500

* For analysis purposes, students were grouped into three groups: (1) heavy users of recreational sports programs and activities -- students who participated at least 25 times a month, (2) light users -- students who participated up to 25 times per month, and (3) nonusers. Heavy users comprised 21% of the students, light users comprised 54% of the students, and nonusers represented 25% of students.

To determine the total buying power from individual students' responses, an estimated average expenditure was calculated for each item. The midpoint of each range of expenditures was used in calculating the estimated average expenditure. Estimated average expenditures were then calculated for heavy, light and nonusers of recreational sports programs and activities. These figures were then extrapolated to the total population of college students to determine the total buying power of participants (heavy and light users) of college recreational sports programs and activities.

Total expenditures for users of college recreational sports programs and activities were $75,766,671,000. Amounts spent on each of 18 items and activities are show in the graphs on pages 188-196. These graphs also show estimated average expenditures for all 18 items for heavy, light and nonusers of recreational sports programs and activities.

Heavy users of recreational sports programs and activities spent considerably more than other students on the following:

- Athletic apparel/clothes
- Athletic shoes
- Clothes, shoes
- Athletic equipment
- Soft drinks, sports drinks
- Personal care, toiletries
- Vitamins, health supplements, health food
- Bottled water
- Videos, movies, DVDs, CDs, headsets
- Sporting events, concerts, clubs
- TVs, radios, stereos
- Travel, vacations
- Alcohol, cigarettes

Higher spending by heavy users of recreational sports can be explained for some of these items by these students' interest in sports (e.g., athletic shoes or even sporting events). Other spending differentials between users and nonusers of recreational sports programs and activities may be explained by the social nature of recreational sports participants. For example, users of recreational sports programs and activities stated that sororities and fraternities, student clubs and organizations, meeting new and different people and social activities were more important determinants of their overall college satisfaction and success than other college students. Nonusers of recreational sports programs and activities outspent users only on car-related expenses.

Total expenditures by users of college recreational sports programs and activities for each item or activity are shown on the table below.

Total expenditures by users of college recreational sports programs	
TOTAL EXPENDITURES BY USERS OF COLLEGE RECREATIONAL SPORTS PROGRAMS	ITEM OR ACTIVITY
$3,953,367,000	Athletic apparel/clothes
$6,795,495,000	Restaurants
$8,724,672,000	Food (grocery stores, convenience stores, etc.)
$7,650,612,000	Cars (gas, repair, etc.)
$2,862,783,000	Athletic shoes
$7,072,272,000	Clothes, shoes (excluding athletic clothes or athletic shoes)
$1,788,723,000	Athletic equipment
$2,106,810,000	Soft drinks, sports drinks
$3,007,368,000	Personal care, toiletries
$2,177,037,000	Vitamins, health supplements, health food
$1,590,435,000	Bottled water
$2,507,517,000	Household items
$2,652,102,000	Videos, movies, DVDs, CDs, headsets, etc.
$2,990,844,000	Sporting events, concerts, clubs, etc.
$2,102,679,000	TVs, radios, stereos
$5,424,003,000	Computers, pagers, CD burners, PDAs, cell phones
$8,633,790,000	Travel/vacation
$3,726,162,000	Alcohol, cigarettes
$75,766,671,000	**Total expenditures** for users of college recreational sports programs

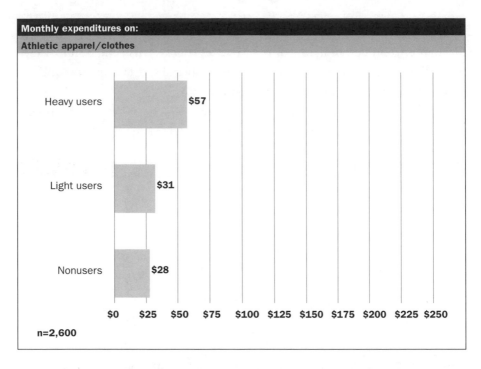

Monthly expenditures on:
Athletic apparel/clothes

- Heavy users: $57
- Light users: $31
- Nonusers: $28

$0 $25 $50 $75 $100 $125 $150 $175 $200 $225 $250

n=2,600

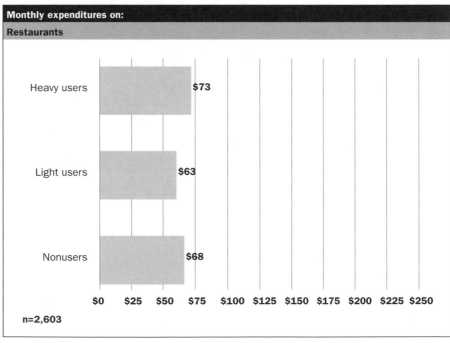

Monthly expenditures on:
Restaurants

- Heavy users: $73
- Light users: $63
- Nonusers: $68

$0 $25 $50 $75 $100 $125 $150 $175 $200 $225 $250

n=2,603

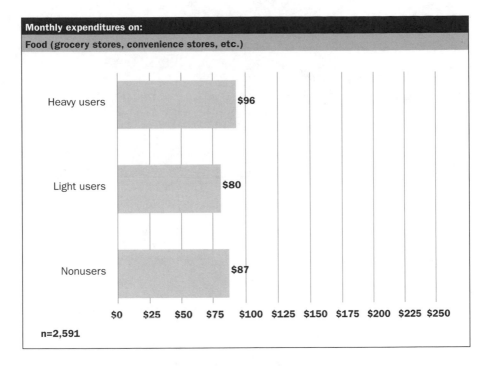

Monthly expenditures on:

Food (grocery stores, convenience stores, etc.)

Heavy users $96

Light users $80

Nonusers $87

$0 $25 $50 $75 $100 $125 $150 $175 $200 $225 $250

n=2,591

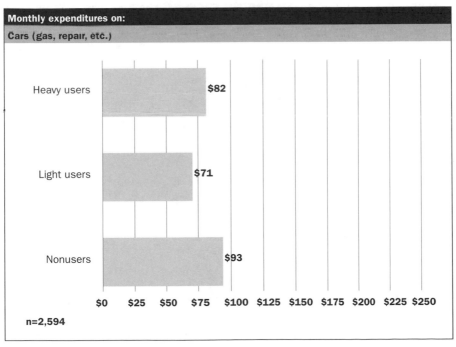

Monthly expenditures on:

Cars (gas, repair, etc.)

Heavy users $82

Light users $71

Nonusers $93

$0 $25 $50 $75 $100 $125 $150 $175 $200 $225 $250

n=2,594

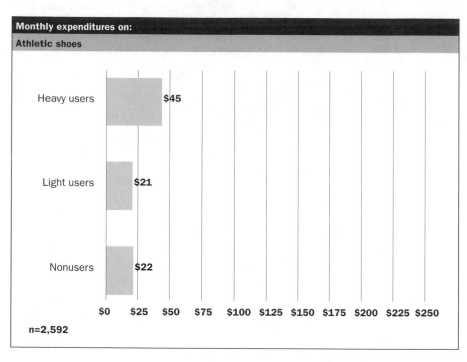

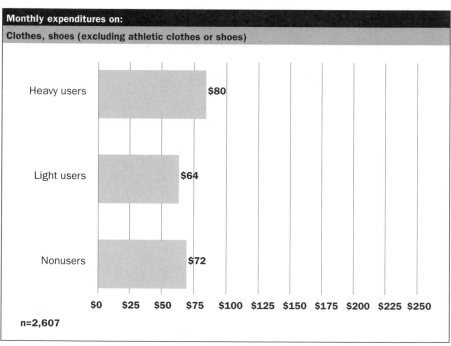

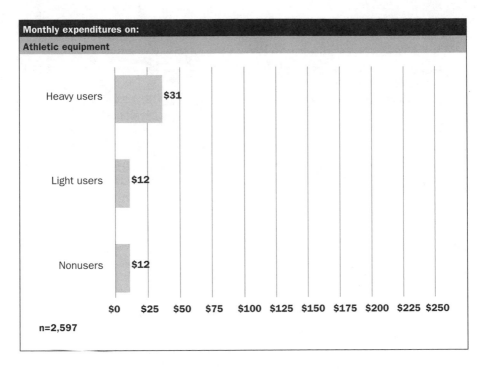

Monthly expenditures on:
Athletic equipment

Heavy users — $31
Light users — $12
Nonusers — $12

$0 $25 $50 $75 $100 $125 $150 $175 $200 $225 $250

n=2,597

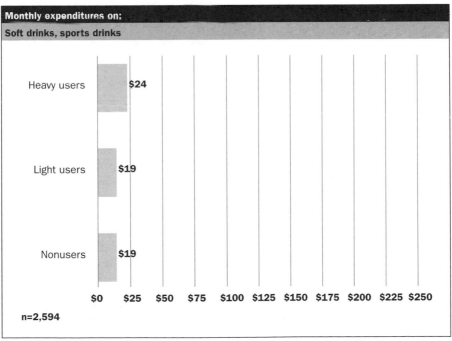

Monthly expenditures on:
Soft drinks, sports drinks

Heavy users — $24
Light users — $19
Nonusers — $19

$0 $25 $50 $75 $100 $125 $150 $175 $200 $225 $250

n=2,594

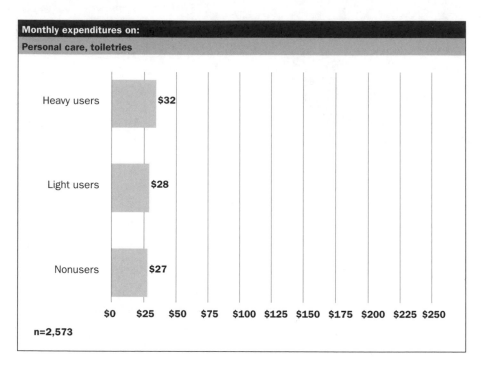

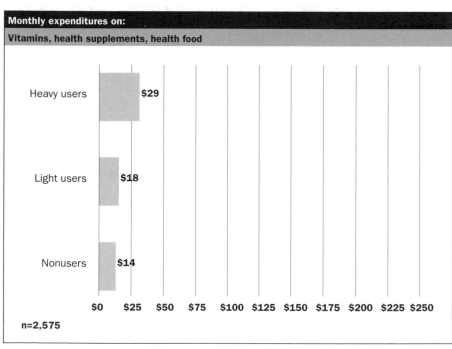

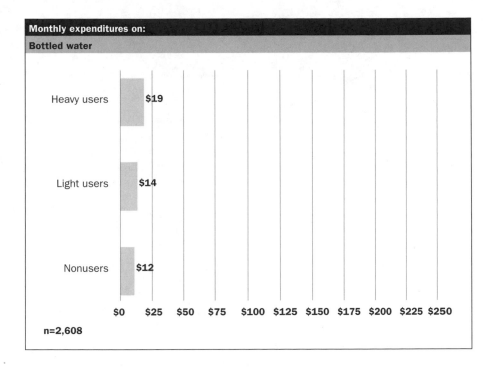

Monthly expenditures on:

Bottled water

Heavy users	$19
Light users	$14
Nonusers	$12

$0 $25 $50 $75 $100 $125 $150 $175 $200 $225 $250

n=2,608

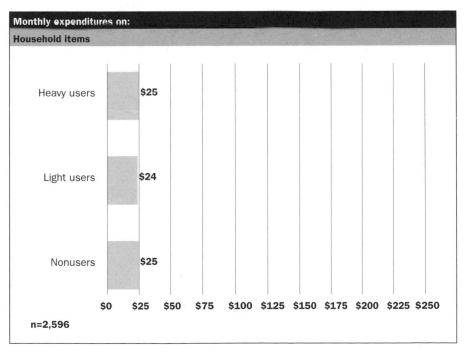

Monthly expenditures on:

Household items

Heavy users	$25
Light users	$24
Nonusers	$25

$0 $25 $50 $75 $100 $125 $150 $175 $200 $225 $250

n=2,596

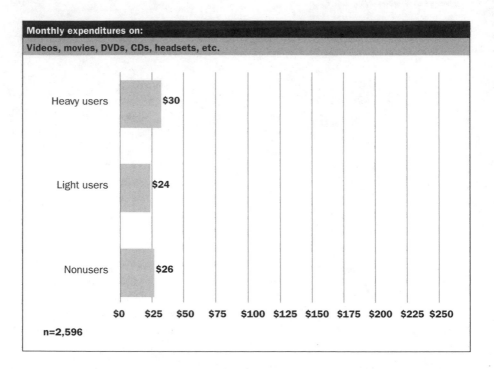

Monthly expenditures on:

Videos, movies, DVDs, CDs, headsets, etc.

Heavy users — $30

Light users — $24

Nonusers — $26

$0 $25 $50 $75 $100 $125 $150 $175 $200 $225 $250

n=2,596

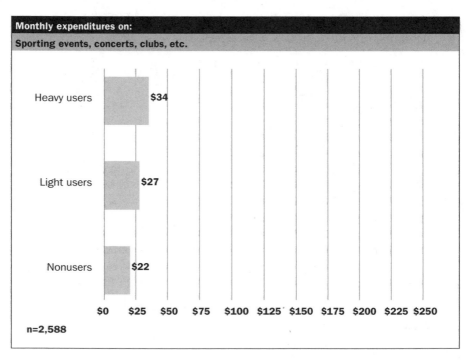

Monthly expenditures on:

Sporting events, concerts, clubs, etc.

Heavy users — $34

Light users — $27

Nonusers — $22

$0 $25 $50 $75 $100 $125 $150 $175 $200 $225 $250

n=2,588

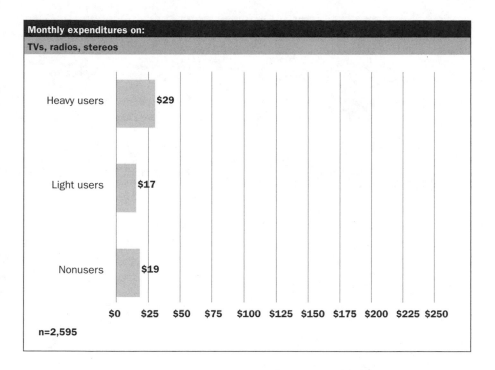

Monthly expenditures on:

TVs, radios, stereos

Heavy users — $29

Light users — $17

Nonusers — $19

$0 $25 $50 $75 $100 $125 $150 $175 $200 $225 $250

n=2,595

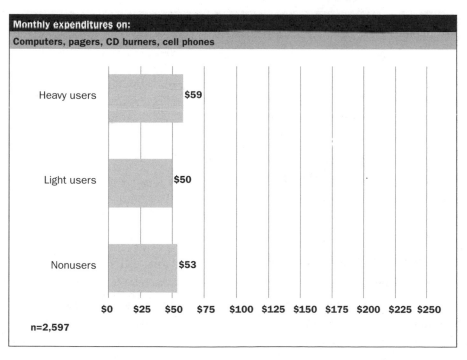

Monthly expenditures on:

Computers, pagers, CD burners, cell phones

Heavy users — $59

Light users — $50

Nonusers — $53

$0 $25 $50 $75 $100 $125 $150 $175 $200 $225 $250

n=2,597

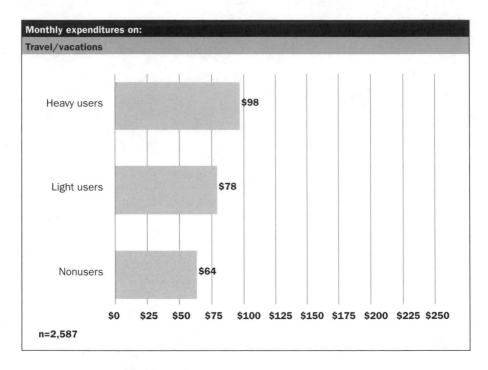

Monthly expenditures on:
Travel/vacations

Heavy users — $98
Light users — $78
Nonusers — $64

$0 $25 $50 $75 $100 $125 $150 $175 $200 $225 $250

n=2,587

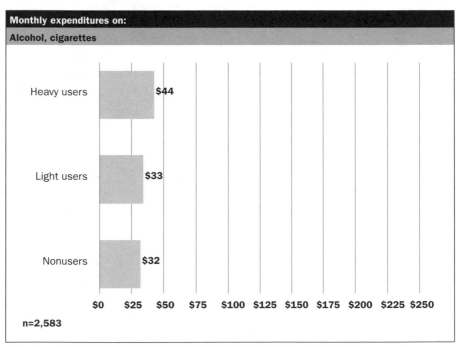

Monthly expenditures on:
Alcohol, cigarettes

Heavy users — $44
Light users — $33
Nonusers — $32

$0 $25 $50 $75 $100 $125 $150 $175 $200 $225 $250

n=2,583

Appendix

Sample of the Recreational Sports Expenditures Survey used in this study.

INSTRUCTIONS: *Please have the Campus Recreation Director or someone who is familiar with budget and spending figures complete this survey. Please answer every single question. You may wish to refer to accounting and budgeting records to complete some questions. You may provide estimates or ranges when completing this survey.*

Please complete this survey by either by mail, fax or online.

1. **Please write in how many years you have worked:**

    _____ In your current position
    _____ At your college/university
    _____ In recreational/intramural sports/activities

2. **Check the responses that reflect how many full-time (FT) and part-time (PT) students attend your college/university.**

FT	PT		FT	PT	
___	___	< 2,500	___	___	10,001 – 15,000
___	___	2,500 – 5,000	___	___	15,001 – 20,000
___	___	5,001 – 7,500	___	___	20,001 – 30,000
___	___	7,501 – 10,000	___	___	Over 30,000

3. **Please write in the number of indoor and outdoor stand-alone and shared (with another discipline, department) recreational centers/complexes your college has. (Write 0 if your college has none.)**

    INDOOR
    _____ # of stand-alone student
    recreation complexes/centers
    _____ # of shared student
    recreation complexes/centers

    OUTDOOR
    _____ # of stand-alone field complexes

    _____ # of shared field complexes

4. **There are 2 major sections for this question: 1 for indoor facilities & 1 for outdoor facilities. For each of these 2 sections, there are 5 items, lettered "A" to "E" on this question. Write all answers on the lines below for your indoor & outdoor facilities.**

A) Please write the year the facilities your campus uses for campus recreation were last built or renovated. (Do NOT include future projects).

B) Write down the approximate cost of the construction or renovation. You may use a range (e.g., $3 to $3.5 million) if you do not have specific numbers.

C) Write an "N" or "R" if you are referencing New construction or Renovation.

D) Add a brief description (e.g., multipurpose center, aquatic center, hockey arena).

E) Write in the gross square footage for each indoor facility and the number of lighted and total number of a flag football sized fields for each outdoor facility.

There are multiple lines to use if your campus has more than 1 recreational facility that has been built or renovated.

INDOOR FACILITIES

A Year Completed	B Approximate Project Cost	C Write "N" or "R"	D Brief Description	E Gross Sq. Ft.
_____	$_____	_____	_____	_____sq. ft.
_____	$_____	_____	_____	_____sq. ft.
_____	$_____	_____	_____	_____sq. ft.
_____	$_____	_____	_____	_____sq. ft.
_____	$_____	_____	_____	_____sq. ft.

OUTDOOR FACILITIES

A Year Completed	B Approximate Project Cost	C Write "N" or "R"	D Brief Description	E Number of Fields (Flag Football Size) Lighted Total
_____	$_____	_____	_____	____ ____
_____	$_____	_____	_____	____ ____
_____	$_____	_____	_____	____ ____
_____	$_____	_____	_____	____ ____
_____	$_____	_____	_____	____ ____

5. **What is included in the indoor facilities your college uses for campus recreation? (Check all that apply.)**

_____ Basketball size courts – How many? _____

_____ Aquatics/pools – How many? _____

_____ Sauna/steam room

_____ First Aid/training room

_____ Free weights/circuit weight training

_____ Jogging track (indoor)

_____ Cardiovascular fitness areas

_____ Inline sports arena

_____ Racquetball/squash courts – How many? _____

_____ Soccer/floor hockey area

_____ Multipurpose rooms – How many? _____

_____ Ice skating/hockey arena or area

_____ Food service

_____ Locker rooms

_____ Maintenance area

_____ Equipment room

_____ Storage

_____ Game rooms – How many? _____

_____ Outdoor pursuit center

_____ Meeting space

_____ Climbing walls – How many? _____

_____ Classrooms

_____ Office space

_____ Laundry room

_____ Bowling alley – # of lanes _____

_____ Child care area

_____ Other _____

_____ Other _____

6.   What is included in the outdoor facilities your college uses for campus recreation? (Check all that apply.)

_____   Basketball size courts – How many? _____

_____   Aquatics/pools – How many? _____

_____   Tennis courts – How many? _____

_____   Ropes course

_____   Bleachers/stands

_____   Jogging track/trail

_____   Public user service space

_____   Skate park, half pipe, etc.

_____   Covered pavilions – How many? _____

_____   Sand volleyball

_____   Waterfront area

_____   Ice skating/hockey arena or area

_____   Food service/concession

_____   Storage

_____   Maintenance area

_____   Equipment room

_____   Other _____

_____   Other _____

7. **This question is for campus recreational facilities planned on your campus for completion within the next 5 years. There are 2 major sections for this question: 1 for indoor facilities & 1 for outdoor facilities. For each of these 2 sections, there are 5 items, lettered "A" to "E" on this question. Write all answers on the lines on the next page for your indoor & outdoor facilities.**

A) Please write the year the facilities will be built or renovated.

B) Write down the approximate cost of the construction or renovation. You may use a range (e.g., $3 to $3.5 million) if you do not have specific numbers.

C) Write an "N" or "R" if you are referencing New construction or Renovation.

D) Add a brief description (e.g., multipurpose center, aquatic center, hockey arena).

E) Write in the gross square footage for each indoor facility and the number of lighted and total number of a flag football-sized fields for each outdoor facility.

There are multiple lines to use if your campus plans to build or renovate more than 1 recreational facility in the next 5 years.

INDOOR FACILITIES

A Year Completed	B Approximate Project Cost	C Write "N" or "R"	D Brief Description	E Gross Sq. Ft.
_____	$_____	_____	_____	_____sq. ft.
_____	$_____	_____	_____	_____sq. ft.
_____	$_____	_____	_____	_____sq. ft.
_____	$_____	_____	_____	_____sq. ft.
_____	$_____	_____	_____	_____sq. ft.

OUTDOOR FACILITIES

A Year Completed	B Approximate Project Cost	C Write "N" or "R"	D Brief Description	E Number of Fields Lighted	Total
_____	$_____	_____	_____	____	____
_____	$_____	_____	_____	____	____
_____	$_____	_____	_____	____	____
_____	$_____	_____	_____	____	____
_____	$_____	_____	_____	____	____

8. **For indoor campus recreational facilities planned on your campus for completion within the next 5 years, please check ( ) what will be included in the constr uction and renovation of your campus' future student recreational facilities?**

_____ Basketball-size courts – How many? _____

_____ Aquatics/pools – How many? _____

_____ Sauna/steam room

_____ First Aid/training room

_____ Free weights/circuit weight training

_____ Jogging track (indoor)

_____ Cardiovascular fitness areas

_____ Inline sports arena

_____ Racquetball/squash courts – How many? _____

_____ Soccer/floor hockey area

_____ Multipurpose rooms – How many? _____

_____ Ice skating/hockey arena or area

_____ Food service

_____ Locker rooms

_____ Maintenance area

_____ Equipment room

_____ Storage

_____ Game rooms – How many? _____

_____ Outdoor pursuit center

_____ Meeting space

_____ Climbing walls – How many? _____

_____ Classrooms

_____ Office space

_____ Laundry room

_____ Bowling alley – # of lanes _____

_____ Child care area

_____ Other _____

_____ Other _____

9   For outdoor campus recreational facilities planned on your campus for completion within the next 5 years, please check ( ) what will be included in the constr uction and renovation of your campus' future student recreational facilities?

_____   Basketball-size courts – How many? _____

_____   Aquatics/pools – How many? _____

_____   Tennis courts – How many? _____

_____   Ropes course

_____   Bleachers/stands

_____   Jogging track/trail

_____   Public user service space

_____   Skate park, half pipe, etc.

_____   Covered pavilions – How many? _____

_____   Sand volleyball

_____   Waterfront area

_____   Ice skating/hockey arena or area

_____   Food service/concession

_____   Storage

_____   Maintenance area

_____   Equipment room

_____   Other _____

_____   Other _____

10. Please write in approximately how much your college has spent for the following recreational sports programs and activities in the most recent fiscal year for each of the following expense categories.

RECREATIONAL SPORTING EQUIPMENT

$ _____   Game/sports equipment (balls, pucks, bats, racquets, gloves, etc.)

$ _____   Goals, nets, mats, pads, etc.

$ _____   Apparel (uniforms, T-shirts, shoes, skates, etc.)

$ _____   Outdoor recreation equipment

$ _____   Other _____

$ _____   Other _____

FACILITIES OPERATIONS

$ _____   Video/audio/entertainment systems, cardio theatre, etc.

$ _____   First Aid, medical supplies

$ _____   Utilities

$ _____   General maintenance & janitorial supplies

$ _____   Floor maintenance, resealing surfaces, carpeting, etc.

$ _____   Field maintenance, fences, backstops, goals, landscaping, etc.

$ _____   Safety & security (alarms, cameras, ID scanners, etc.)

$ _____   Facility components (standards, backboards, timing devices, bleachers, etc.)

$ _____   Other _____

$ _____   Other _____

ADMINISTRATION

$ _____   Computers/software/technical

$ _____   Marketing/promotions/incentives.

$ _____   Office supplies/equipment

$ _____   Consultants/contractual services

$ _____   Salaries & wages

$ _____   Dues, memberships, publications

$ _____   Other _____

$ _____   Other _____

MISCELLANEOUS

$ _____   Appliances/furniture

$ _____   Child care facilities/services

$ _____   Travel (transportation, accommodations, food)

$ _____   Other _____

11. **There are certain expenditures that occur infrequently such as buying free weight equipment or cardiovascular equipment. Please write down the total dollar amount your recreational sports department has spent on these infrequently purchased items over the past 10 years. You can approximate or use ranges.**

$ _____ Free weights/weight training circuit equipment

$ _____ Video/audio/entertainment systems, cardio theatre, electronics

$ _____ Cardiovascular equipment

$ _____ Laundry & maintenance equipment

$ _____ Misc. facility equipment (standards, goals, netting, padding, backboards, curtains, etc.)

$ _____ Resurfacing (courts, lanes, rooms, etc.)

$ _____ Architectural services

$ _____ Aquatics equipment

$ _____ Lighting

$ _____ Other infrequent purchases _____

$ _____ Other infrequent purchases _____

12. **For these same infrequently purchased items, please write down the total amount your recreational sports department plans to spend for these items over the next 5 years. You can approximate or use ranges.**

$ _____ Free weights/weight training circuit equipment

$ _____ Video/audio/entertainment systems, cardio theatre, electronics

$ _____ Cardiovascular equipment

$ _____ Laundry & maintenance equipment

$ _____ Misc. facility equipment (standards, goals, netting, padding, backboards, curtains, etc.)

$ _____ Resurfacing (courts, lanes, rooms, etc.)

$ _____ Architectural services

$ _____ Aquatics equipment

$ _____ Lighting

$ _____ Other infrequent purchases _____

$ _____ Other infrequent purchases _____

13. **Do you have food service (including vending machines) as part of your campus recreation, and if so, is it outsourced or handled in-house?**

_____ Do not have food service (SKIP TO 16)

_____ Outsource all food service

_____ Outsource some food service – handle some food service in-house

_____ Handle all food service in-house

14. **Please estimate the revenue your department received from food service in the past fiscal year.**

$ _____ Revenue from company to which you outsourced food service operations

$ _____ Direct sales from food service operations handled in-house

15. **Please check ( ) the items you sell as par t of your food service operation – DOUBLE check ( ) the 3 items for which you think unit sales are highest.**

_____ Sandwiches, wraps, etc.

_____ Fruit drinks, smoothies, health drinks, etc.

_____ Ice cream, yogurt, etc.

_____ Health bars, energy bars, etc.

_____ Soft drinks

_____ Candy

_____ Salads

_____ Soup, chili, etc.

_____ Fresh fruit

_____ Chips, pretzels, etc.

_____ Breads, rolls, etc.

_____ Coffee, tea, milk

_____ Pizza, pasta

_____ Bottled water

_____ Other _____

16. **Please write in your college's total (capital, operational and all other) budgets this year for recreational sports. You can approximate or use ranges.**

$ _____ Capital budget
$ _____ Operational budget
$ _____ All other budgets
$ _____ Total budget (sum of the first 3)

17. **Does your facility allow paid promotional signs and boards indoors or outdoors?**

YES NO
_____ _____ Allow paid outdoor signs/boards
_____ _____ Allow paid indoor signs/boards

18. **We are interested in learning who has purchasing authority for recreational sports purchases at your college and learning if there are maximum expenditures for which this person can make decisions. Please**

A) Check ( ) each job title/position that exists at y our college,
B) Check ( ) if each le vel has purchasing authority for your college's recreational sports purchases, and
C) Write in the maximum dollar amount of purchase over which this person has for a single purchase. (If "No Limit," please write NL)

JOB TITLE/POSITION	PURCHASING AUTHORITY		MAXIMUM PURCHASE AUTHORIZATION
	YES	NO	
_____ Director of Recreational Sports	_____	_____	$_____
_____ Associate Director	_____	_____	$_____
_____ Assistant Director	_____	_____	$_____
_____ Coordinator	_____	_____	$_____
_____ Other_____	_____	_____	$_____

19. **In which state is your college located?**

_____

20. **Please write in your name and email/fax information in case we need to ask you a question about any of the information you have provided. Your answers will be treated confidentially and not viewed by anyone outside the researchers.**

Your name _____

Fax number _____

Email address _____

Thank you for participating in this important NIRSA project.

Existing Indoor Facility Descriptions (451)

Athletic building/recreational center (175)
- 110,000 recreation (renovation to athletics)
- 35,000 square feet (dedicated) for recreation/convention center
- Academic, multiuse
- Adams center intramurals/concerts/athletics
- Administration areas, classrooms, etc.
- Athletic complex (3)
- Campus recreation facility
- Campus recreation
- Coliseum
- Combination of athletic, academic and recreational complex
- Comprehensive recreation center
- Fitness and recreation center (3)
- Fitness center (13)
- Fitness center/classrooms
- Fitness/recreation/wellness center
- Health and sports center
- Health science, fitness facility
- HPAB complex
- HPER Center
- Installed large fitness center
- KFC (fitness center)
- Kiewit Fitness Center
- Multipurpose arena
- Multipurpose bowling and billiards; office
- Multipurpose center (56)
- Multipurpose center (fitness activities & intramural sports)
- Multipurpose center/locker room (2)
- Multipurpose facility (5)
- Multipurpose gym (3)
- Multipurpose recreation facility shared with academics
- Multipurpose recreation & athletic building (2)
- Multipurpose recreation center (7)
- New and renovated multipurpose facility
- New indoor complex
- New wrestling room and fitness center renovation
- Outdoor center
- Outdoor recreation building
- PE center
- Petersen Events Center and student recreation center
- Recreation building (2)
- Recreation center (13)
- Recreation offices
- Recreational center and renovation
- Recreational sports center/multipurpose center
- Renovate multipurpose center (3)
- Renovation of athletic facilities/new construction of recreational center
- Renovation of fitness center (2)
- Shared multipurpose center
- Shared PEHR/athletic/campus recreation
- Shared recreation building with PE
- Shooting range for ROTC and offices for them as well
- Student activity center - not all recreation sports
- Student fitness center
- Student pavilion indoor court space
- Student recreation center addition – cardio and weight
- Student recreation center (14)
- Student recreational center primarily fitness space

- Temporary recreation center
- Two multipurpose rooms
- Union/recreational space
- Wellness center/student center

Gym (48)
- Ball gym renovations
- Bear Down Gym, multipurpose facility with locker rooms and classrooms and office space, also used by another department
- Converted space to gym
- Four gyms (2)
- Gregory Gym renovation
- Gym – weight room
- Gym (1 gym floor with stage, 4 exercise areas, 3 rest rooms, 2 locker rooms, bleachers on each side)
- Gym (14)
- Gym center
- Gym renovation
- Gymnasium (5)
- Gyms
- Main gymnasium (3)
- Multipurpose gym
- Not shared facility houses 5 gymnasium spaces
- PE gymnasium
- Relight & repair old gym
- Remodeled 1915 gym
- Renovating old campus school gym
- Replace gymnasium floor
- Schreiber gym
- Seven gyms
- Small gym (2)
- Three gyms (2)
- Two gyms
- Two gyms, exercise area

Pool/Aquatic center (45)
- Aquatic and fitness center

- Aquatic (4)
- Aquatic center (6)
- Aquatic center 50m
- Aquatic center: 50m pool & diving well
- Arena/aquatic center
- Grizzly pool
- Indoor pool (3)
- New pool
- Outdoor swimming pool
- Pool (22)
- Swimming pools
- Two pools, one gym
- Watatorium

Gym oriented equipment (weights, aerobic rooms, etc.) (42)
- 11,000 square foot weight room
- 6,500 square feet weight room
- Added aerobics studio
- Addition to SRC (weight & exercise)
- Aerobics (3)
- Aerobics classes
- Aerobics room
- Aerobics room, locker rooms
- Aerobics studio
- Cardiovascular
- Dance
- Dorm 24-hour weight room
- Dorm weight room
- Fitness and weight room
- Fitness studio, cardio
- Group exercise room
- Group exercise room, weight room
- Martial arts, spinning activity room
- Nautilus equipment
- Racquetball conversion to weight room
- Two aerobic/dance studios
- Two multipurpose rooms
- Weight room (12)

- Weight room equipment and floor
- Weight room, aerobic room
- Weight room, cardio, wellness
- Weight room (redesign)
- Weight, cardio
- Weight, cardio and aerobics

Field house (20)
- Field house (10)
- Field house upgrade
- Field house, athletic offices
- Hollinger Field House
- Multipurpose field house (2)
- New field house
- Old gym/field house (2)
- Renovation of field house
- UWF Field House

Racquetball courts (19)
- 14 racquetball courts
- 15 racquetball courts, six squash courts
- Four racquetball courts
- Racquetball courts (13)
- Squash courts
- Two racquetball courts (2)

Basketball arena/courts (18)
- Arena (2)
- Basketball arena (4)
- Basketball court (2)
- Basketball courts (3)
- Five courts
- New wood basketball floor (2)
- Three court gym
- Three multipurpose courts
- Two basketball
- Worthen Arena

Additional space or general/ unspecified renovations (15)
- Add 77,000 square feet - renovate some old areas

- Add-on to current building
- Added about 3,000 feet to locker area to pool
- Addition - locker rooms
- Addition and renovation
- Additional 45,000 square feet
- Expansion of 1995 center
- Expansion to recreational center
- JWC Building addition
- Remodel existing facility (2)
- Remodel locker rooms/office
- Renovate a carriage house to an outing rental center (annex)
- Renovated locker room and gym remodeling
- Various updates

Track (13)
- Indoor track (3)
- Jogging track
- Raised 3 lane jogging track
- Repair indoor track
- Resurface track
- Track (5)
- Training track

Tennis courts (7)
- Four covered tennis courts
- Indoor tennis courts (2)
- Tennis center
- Tennis courts (3)

Hockey/ice skating arena (6)
- Ice rink (2)
- Hockey
- Hockey arena
- Ice arena
- Ice arena - 2 rinks

Other (43)
- Accessibility improvement/new lobby & service desk – MCV campus

- Air filtration system in pool
- Air structure over football field
- Archery
- Bowling center
- Classrooms (3)
- Climbing
- Climbing wall (4)
- Combative room
- Design
- Dome roof renovation
- Dome stadium
- Don't have this info on file
- Faculty locker room accessibility and office renovations – MCV campus
- Floor covering
- Game room
- Healthsouth Physical Therapy
- HPER Complex
- IM East
- Indoor soccer
- Lights for all fields
- New floor in arena
- New golf shop
- New snack bar – sell at athletic events
- Office
- Offices, classrooms
- Offices, lab
- Olympics
- Outdoor center, office and storage space
- Outdoor program area, training room, administration area
- Renovated barn into climbing gym
- Rock wall
- Roller hockey
- Shared university coliseum
- Shower renovations – Cary St.
- Sylvania campus was built
- There is also a small food court and study lounge
- Volleyball courts

Existing Outdoor Facility Descriptions (299)

Multipurpose field (99)
- Artificial turf field (3)
- Athletic fields (2)
- Auxiliary field
- Cooke field
- Dewitt cabin/club fields
- Dornblazer sports fields
- Environmental clean-up (will be athletic fields)
- Expanded natural turf fields
- Field (2)
- Field complex
- Field with parking structure below
- Fields
- Four fields, no lights
- Grass fields (2)
- Green space, 6.5 acres
- Large open area
- Lighted multipurpose
- Multipurpose grass fields
- Multipurpose – softball/soccer
- Multipurpose – softball/soccer/ tennis
- Multipurpose complex (2)
- Multipurpose facility for flag football, softball and soccer
- Multipurpose field/softball diamond
- Multipurpose fields (27)
- Multipurpose fields with backstop
- Multipurpose green field with bleachers (2)
- Multipurpose pavilion built by architectural students as part of a class. They also designed it with a classroom, office, 2 storage areas (1 climate controlled), covered patio, maintenance closet and restrooms.

- Multipurpose turf area and grass field
- New and renovated field
- North campus playing fields
- North recreation field
- One multipurpose field with lights that is fenced in and located in the center of campus
- One partially lighted large field area
- Open field space (3)
- Outdoor athletic fields/tennis courts
- Outdoor course
- Outdoor fields (3)
- Outdoor fields 2 artificial turf
- Outdoor sports center
- Playing fields (5)
- Recreation fields (3)
- Riverbowl sports fields
- Six field complex for intramural and sport club use
- Smaller field and lights, parking lot, bathroom and office
- South recreation field
- Sports club field
- Synthetic fields
- Tennis courts
- Three multipurpose fields
- Turf field (3)
- Two outdoor fields
- Two sites totaling 32 acres/ multipurpose IM and Sport Club
- Two synthetic fields
- Various fields

Fields designated for a specific sport (i.e. football, softball, etc.) (74)
- Athletic field hockey/recreation sports turf field
- Athletic fields

- Baseball & softball new artificial turf
- Baseball complex
- Baseball field (3)
- Basketball volleyball roller hockey
- Equivalent of 22 soccer fields
- Fields for flag football and softball (2)
- Flag football field (4)
- Flag football fields (2)
- Football field (2)
- Football field, softball field (2)
- Football practice field
- Football stadium
- Football, soccer
- Four flag football
- Four football
- Four lighted playfields
- Four softball, 1 baseball
- Outdoor fields - two football, one soccer
- Press box/softball
- Shared facility with athletics, 2 Astroturf field areas
- Soccer and baseball fields
- Soccer field (11)
- Soccer, rugby, lacrosse, frisbee (2)
- Softball & soccer complex
- Softball field (16)
- Softball fields/picnic park, restrooms
- Softball, soccer, football
- Softball/football complex (3)
- Sports club use, 2 soccer fields (full size)
- Stadium
- Three softball diamonds
- Two flag football fields (2)
- Two flag football fields, 1 soccer field
- Two full-size soccer fields, 4 football fields

Tennis court(s) (26)
- 10 tennis courts
- 12 tennis courts (2)
- Eight tennis courts (3)
- Four tennis courts (2)
- Outdoor pavilion
- Outdoor tennis courts (2)
- Recreational tennis courts
- Tennis complex
- Tennis courts (13)

Lighting (15)
- Lighted one playing field
- Lighted outdoor fields
- Lighted turf fields
- Lighting (2)
- Lighting for fields & courts
- Lighting for fields (3)
- Lights (2)
- Lights installed
- New lights (2)
- Three lighted softball

Track (15)
- 400-meter track
- Astro Turf field/track
- New track
- Outdoor jogging track
- Running track
- Shared facility, 1 small grass field existed, added hammer throw cage for varsity track
- Track (7)
- Track and field arena area
- Track and field stadium

Intramural Field (14)
- Intramural and club field (2)
- Intramural field (10)
- New intramural field
- Three intramural fields

Sand volleyball (8)
- Sand volleyball courts (3)
- Three sand volleyball courts
- Two sand volleyball courts (3)
- Volleyball courts

Resurfacing of field/track/course (8)
- Artificial surface
- Artificial turf replacement 116,000 square feet
- Bermuda grass installed
- Reseed fields
- Reseed, new face, remove softball, multi-sport fields
- Sand-based, sport grass
- Tennis courts resurfacing
- Turf and track renovation

Basketball court(s) (7)
- Three blacktop basketball courts
- Three basketball courts
- Basketball courts (5)

Practice field(s) (5)
- Practice baseball field
- Practice fields (2)
- Practice soccer fields
- Practice/intramural fields

Rope course (5)
- Bike trails and ropes course
- Ropes course (4)

Pool (3)
- Outdoor pool
- Pool
- Swimming pool

Golf (3)
- Former golf course
- Golf course (2)

Other (17)
- Academic and recreational space
- Additional waterfront
- All fields leased from parks or high schools
- Challenge course
- Fitness trail
- Gazebo with bathrooms
- Inline rink
- Irrigated fields
- Irrigation, skimmed fields
- Lakeside camping
- Leveled, irrigation system, drainage system
- New complex
- Outdoor complex
- Park
- Sylvania campus was built
- Trails system upgrade
- Two horseshoe areas

Planned Indoor Facility Descriptions (142)

Athletic building/recreational center/multipurpose center (39)
- Athletic annex
- Campus recreation center
- Cardio, outdoor pursuits, food service, multipurpose
- Dedicated recreation space, multipurpose court, outing center
- Field house with offices, training room storage
- Gym space – multipurpose and weight room space
- Multicourt recreation building
- Multipurpose activity room
- Multipurpose center (7)
- Multipurpose facility (2)
- Multipurpose, athletic arena

- New & renovated recreation space
- New recreational center (3)
- Phillips hall multipurpose
- Recreation park and fitness complex
- Recreation/kinesiology facility
- Recreational sport building addition
- Sports field complex
- Stand along recreation center
- Student recreation center (8)
- Wellness center (2)
- Wellness/multi-purpose complex

Addition/Renovation to an existing building/area (33)
- Addition and renovation of fitness
- Addition to existing facility
- Addition to weight room
- Aquatics complex/renovate existing indoor pool
- Building addition
- Building renovation and seismic improvement (2)
- Convocation, dining - recreation
- Exercise area, game room
- Existing field house
- Expanded fitness area
- Expanded office space
- Expansion of gym
- Expansion of multipurpose center
- Expansion to field house
- Expansion/renovation of recreation center (2)
- Fitness center expansion
- Flooring, ceiling lights
- Locker rooms renovated (2)
- Meeting room conversion to fitness/multipurpose
- New gym floor
- Recreation center expansion, mostly fitness

- Renovate 1934 gym building
- Renovate building add more space
- Renovated the rest of facility
- Renovation and expansion
- Resurface indoor running track
- Roof replacement
- Student recreation center addition/ expansion
- Turf field area
- Two courts added

Fitness Center (14)
- Cardio
- Fitness area
- Fitness center (3)
- Fitness center in a new student union
- Fitness complex in commons building
- Fitness facility
- Fitness room
- Fitness satellite area
- Fitness/free weight/cardio rooms, storage and locker rooms
- Fitness/weight room
- New carpeting/floor surface in fitness center
- Satellite fitness center

Aquatic Center/Pool (12)
- Aquatic center (3)
- Construct three new outdoor pools
- Indoor pool
- New aquatics complex
- Pool (4)
- Pool deck and party space
- Swimming pool

Climbing wall (8)
- Climbing wall (6)
- Indoor climbing wall
- Indoor climbing wall installation

Gym (type not mentioned) (5)
- Campus school gymnasium
- Gym/stage for concerts
- Gyms
- Redo gym
- Three court gym

Racquetball courts (4)
- Racquetball
- Racquetball courts
- Racquetball courts (2) conversion to multipurpose room
- Two racquetball courts

Basketball arena/courts (4)
- Arena stadium for basketball team
- Basketball
- Four basketball courts (2)

Aerobic/dance rooms (4)
- Dance facility
- Aerobics rooms (3)

Weight room (3)
- Auxiliary weight room
- Weights
- Weight room

Hockey (2)
- Hockey arena (2)

Tennis (1)
- Indoor Tennis

Other (13)
- Air conditioning in gym and fitness center area
- Air inflated cover over outdoor multipurpose turf football/soccer facility
- Built an indoor track
- Classrooms office building

- Jogging lanes
- Locker room, classroom
- Office renovation and computer wiring
- Outdoor center
- Running track
- Softball/tennis locker building
- Student ref proposed
- Support building for 2 filed spaces
- The Massari Arena

Planned Outdoor Facility Descriptions (113)

Multipurpose field (29)
- Astro Turf playing field
- Club sport and athletic track/field practice area
- Design multipurpose field and park in the future
- Eight acre field development
- Field
- Intramural fields (2)
- Multipurpose fields (7)
- Multipurpose fields (artificial)
- Multipurpose football, soccer, rugby, lacrosse
- Multipurpose stadium
- Multipurpose trail
- Multipurpose, football and soccer
- Multiuse field for football and softball
- Multiuse turf field
- Natural grass field
- One meter field
- Park, pavilion playground area
- Playing field
- Practice/intramural field
- Sports fields
- Two fields (2)

Fields designated for a specific sport (i.e. football, softball, etc.) (15)
- Athletic fields, intramural fields
- Ball field clay and sand
- Baseball field/park
- Fields football and softball
- Flag football
- Flag football/softball
- Four softball fields
- Soccer field (2)
- Softball and football complex
- Softball field (2)
- Softball, soccer, football
- Softball/football field
- Turf football field

Resurfacing of field/track/course (13)
- Cary St. artificial turf replacement, pad & sub-surface repairs - pending approval (funds are already available)
- Grade/reseed field
- Improvements to existing fields
- Install field turf or large outdoor field
- New & renovated multipurpose field with synthetic turf
- Renovate field areas at the Gazebo Recreation Area with piping a ditch, reconfiguring of the fields
- Renovate fields
- Renovate grass fields
- Replace St. Pan fields
- Reseeding
- Synthetic field
- Synthetic fields
- Turf fields

Pool (7)
- 50 meter outdoor pool with spa
- Aquatic center (2)
- Leisure pool
- Outdoor leisure pool
- Pool
- Swimming pool

Tennis court(s) (6)
- 12 tennis courts
- Eight tennis
- Tennis center
- Tennis
- Tennis/club sport complex
- Courts

Lighting (6)
- Installing the lighting
- Light field
- Light fields
- Light six sand volleyball courts
- Lighted playing fields
- Stadium lights

Sand Volleyball (5)
- Volleyball courts
- Sand volleyball court (4)

Basketball court(s) (5)
- Basketball (2)
- Two basketball
- One basketball court
- Outdoor basketball

Rope course (5)
- High ropes course
- Ropes course (4)

Track (3)
- Running track
- Track (2)

Climbing wall (1)
- Outdoor climbing wall

Renovation to an existing building (1)
- Sports equipment building

Golf (1)
- Golf range

Other (16)
- 345 acre camp development
- Archery
- Covered pavilion (2)
- Fill low fields, redress/crown
- Hockey
- Horseshoes
- Ice rink
- Inline skate
- Jogging trail
- Nine acre field with parking structure below
- Outdoor storage shed
- Picnic area
- Skate park
- University park with picnic areas, waterfront
- Waterfront nature park

Bibliography

Astin, A.W. (1968). *The College Environment.* Washington, D.C.: American Council on Education.

Astin, A.W. (1975). *Preventing Students from Dropping Out. San Francisco*: Jossey-Bass.

Astin, A.W. (1977). *Four Critical Years.* San Francisco: Jossey-Bass.

Astin, A.W. (1984). Student involvement: A developmental theory for higher education. *Journal of College Student Personnel,* XXV, 297-308.

Astin, A.W. (1993). *What matters in college?: Four critical years revisited.* San Francisco: Jossey-Bass.

Belch, H., Gebel, M. & Maas, G. (2001). Relationship Between Student Recreation Complex Use, Academic Performance, and Persistence of First-Time Freshmen. *NASPA Journal, XXXVIII,* 254-266.

Berg, J.O. (1970). Differences Between Male Participants and Non-Participants in a College Intramural Sports Program in Regard to Academic Achievement and Academic Ability. *21st Annual Conference Proceedings of the National Intramural Association,* pp.80-88.

Biddulph, L.G. (1954). Athletic Achievement and the Personal and Social Adjustment of High School Boys. *Research Quarterly,* XXV, 1-7.

Booth, E.G., Jr. (1958). Personality Traits of Athletes as Measured by the MMPI. *Research Quarterly,* XXIX, 127-39.

Buccholz, D. (1993). *Evaluation of recreational sports facilities and programs at Arizona State University.* Unpublished master's thesis, Arizona State University, 1993.

Diener, E., Emmons, R.A., Larsen, R.J. & Griffin, S. (1985). The Satisfaction With Life Scale. *Journal of Personality Assessment,* 49, 71-75.

Hackensmith, C.W., and Miller, L. (1938). A Comparison of Academic Grades and Intelligence Scores of Participants and Non-Participants in Intramural Athletics at the University of Kentucky. *Research Quarterly,* IX, 94-99.

Hesel, Richard A. (2000). Intercollegiate athletics have little influence on college choice – Intramural and recreational opportunities matter more. *Student Poll*. IV, 1-12. Art and Science Group, Baltimore, MD.

Kroll, W. and Peterson, K.H. (1965). Personality Factor Profiles of Collegiate Football Teams. *Research Quarterly*, XXXVI, 433-40.

Light, R.J. (1990). *The Harvard Assessment Seminars: Explorations with Students and Faculty about Teaching, Learning and Student Life*. Cambridge, MA: Harvard University Graduate School of Education and Kennedy School of Government.

Maas, G. (1999). *Relationship Between Campus Recreation Participation and Measures of College Success*. Presented at the 50th Annual Conference of the National Intramural Recreational Sports Association. Milwaukee, Wisconsin.

Merriman, J.B. (May, 1960). Relationship of Personality Traits to Motor Ability. *Research Quarterly*, XXXI , 163-73.

Mendell, E.R. (1973). *Differences Between College Male intramural Participants and Non-Participants with Regard to Personality, Athletic Background, and Certain Scholastic Indices*. UMI Dissertation Services: University of Southern Mississippi.

Pascarella, E., & Terenzini, P. (1977). Patterns of student-faculty informal interaction beyond the classroom and voluntary freshman attrition. *Journal of Higher Education*, XXXXVIII, 540-552.

Ragheb, M. and McKinney, J. (1993). Campus Recreation and Perceived Academic Stress. *Journal of College Student Development*. XXXIIII, 5-10.

Rarick, L. (1943). A Survey of Athletic Participation and Scholastic Achievement. *Journal of Educational Research*, XXXVII 174-80.

Ryan, F.J. (1990). *Influences of Intercollegiate Athletic Participation on the Psychosocial Development of College Students*. UMI Dissertation Services: University of California, Los Angeles.

Ryan, R.R. (1963). *The Effects of Participation in Selected Intramural Sports Upon Physical Fitness, Social and Emotional Adjustment of College Fraternity Men*. UMI Dissertation Services: Colorado State College.

Smith, M.K. and Thomas, J. (1989). The Relationship of College Outcomes to Post-Graduate Success. *Assessment of Student Outcome in Higher Education.* Knoxville: The University of Tennessee, Center for Assessment Research and Development.

Sperling, A.P. (1942). The Relationship Between Personality Adjustment and Achievement in Physical Education Activities. *Research Quarterly,* XIII, 351-354.

Terenzini, P. & Pascarella, E. (1977). Voluntary freshman attrition and patterns of social and academic integration in a university: A test of a conceptual model. *Research in Higher Education,* XV, 109-27.

Varca, P., Shaffer, G. & Sanders, V. (1984). A longitudinal investigation of sport participation and life satisfaction. *Journal of Sport Psychology,* VI, 440-447.

Wade, B.K. (1991). *A profile of the real world of undergraduate students and how they spend discretionary time.* Paper presented at the Annual Meeting of the American Educational Research Association (Chicago). ERIC Document Reproduction Service No. ED 33 7776).

Washington State University (2001). Student Recreation Center User Data. Unpublished.

Washke, P.R. (1940). A Study of Intramural Sports Participation and Scholastic Attainment. *Research Quarterly,* XI, 22-27.

Werner, A.C., and Gottheil, E. (March, 1966) Personality Development and Participation in College Athletics. Research Quarterly, XXXVII, 126-31.